CW00595214

The Complete Cheese Pairing *Cookbook*

The Complete Cheese Pairing
Cookbook

MORGAN MCGLYNN CARR

WHITE LION
PUBLISHING

Georgie Rose, thank you for keeping me company whilst writing this book and giving me a gentle kick when I needed to get on with it. I love you more than I can put into words. Mum x

Contents

INTRODUCTION TO CHEESE PAIRING   **6**

What is cheese pairing   8

What makes a cheese cheesy?   10

How do we taste?   16

Find your inner fromager   18

Pair like a pro   20

How to use the charts   22

CHEESE PAIRING CHARTS   **24**

My favourites   26

Cheese and food pairing   30

Cheese and drink pairing   98

World cheese pairings   124

Cheese pairing for the seasons   160

200 ULTIMATE CHEESE PAIRINGS   **194**

Index   202

Acknowledgements   206

Introduction to cheese pairing

For me, cheese is one of life's greatest pleasures. Born out of necessity – to preserve milk as a longer-lasting, nourishing food source, after the milk itself had soured to become undrinkable – cheese now appears in thousands of incredible varieties from all over the world. Every cheese tells a story – the tasting experience in a single bite captures a place, time and artistry: the flavours of a Tête de Moine pay homage to monastic cheesemakers in the Alps; a farmhouse Cheddar emerges steeped in the history of generations of family cheesemakers, whose cows graze on the pastures of the English countryside. And many more stories besides.

But, unless you are a caseophile (a cheese connoisseur), I totally understand that a packed cheese-shop counter can be a little overwhelming. There will be cheeses with names that seem almost unpronounceable; cheeses that smell worse than my husband's football kit after training; cheeses that are every shade of cream and yellow, or flecked with blue or green; cheeses that are oozy or firm, coated in ash, wrapped in wax or encased in rind – and the decisions on what to choose can seem mind-boggling to make. I get it. But, I firmly believe that discovering cheese will be the greatest hobby you could ever take up. And, with this book in one hand, you'll learn not just about the cheeses themselves, but about the pairings that bring out the best in them.

I started my cheese shop in London at just 19 years old, armed with a passion for and commitment to specialist cheese. Now, I have lived, breathed, made, tasted, judged and written about cheese for over 17 years. I think it's safe to say I'm a big fan! From the very beginning, my aim has been to find the world's best-made and most interesting cheeses and to share them with as many people as possible.

After all these years of being a cheesemonger, I am acutely aware that the stunning artisan and farmhouse cheeses from across the world are more than good enough on their own. But, imagine a world where they could be even better?

Where every flavour in them could pop, every texture yield, and every mouthful make the next one unwaveringly irresistible. That world is the world of delicious cheese pairing – the process of partnering different cheeses with jams, nuts, fruit, meats, and myriad other foods (and drinks, too). Every pairing is greater than the sum of its parts: it brings contrast, harmony, and a tasting experience that is often not only amazing, but also unexpected – in the best of ways.

For me, finding a new, exciting cheese and experimenting to find my perfect pair for it never feels like work. And there are no rights and wrongs. While there will be underlying flavour profiles that you might expect from a particular style of cheese or a particular region, and pointers I can give for what to look out for in each pairing, our individual experience of a cheese pair will be unique. There will be some pairings that I love that you can take or leave. And your favourites may not be mine. This is a culinary adventure – we are on it together, but how we each interpret and remember it, and the experience we take forward from it, is ours alone. Once you embrace that individuality and have confidence in it, any notion of cheese pairing being overwhelming or intimidating melts away – leaving only the fun.

This book is all about giving you the roadmap to travel your own cheese-pairing journey. It begins with a few guiding principles to help you on your way, but it's in the experimentation – the steps you take with the boards in front of you – that the fun really starts. Throughout, the pairing boards will help you to see for yourself how to bring flavours, textures and aromas together for an incredible cheesy experience. After each board are two (sometimes three) recipes – some of which demonstrate how you can use the knowledge you've gained in your pairing journey in your cooking; and some of which enable you to make your own pairs. By the time you reach the end of the book, you will be a seasoned cheese expert who can regale friends and lovers with your pairing knowledge and impress with your perfectly paired cheeseboards and dishes. I can't wait to hear all about it!

Happy pairing!

What is cheese pairing?

At its simplest, cheese pairing is the art of combining different types of cheese with complementary foods and drinks to enhance the overall taste experience.

The aim is to find a perfect match that either brings out the flavour and texture qualities in both the cheese and its pairing partner, or elevates our experience of the cheese to new heights. The pairing might occur on a cheeseboard, or it might be because the cheese and its specific pair make the perfect complement as ingredients in a single recipe for another dish – combining an aged Cheddar cheese with apple cider, say, to create the ultimate mac 'n' cheese (see page 112). This book brims with both boards and recipes that demonstrate just how versatile and magical cheese pairing can be.

To really understand cheese pairing, it's important to consider what it is to taste a cheese. Flavour, aroma, texture, intensity and finish all play their part in how we decide what makes a good pairing. In choosing the best pair, every one of these dimensions of our experience of a cheese matters:

Flavour takes centre stage – every cheese has a unique profile that ranges from mild and creamy, like a Chaource, to sharp and tangy, like an aged Cheddar; or deep and earthy, like a Camembert, to light and floral, like a mountain goat's cheese.

Aroma is the gateway to the cheese's flavour. Smelling wakes up not just your sense of smell, but also your sense of taste, because the two are inextricably linked (see page 16).

Texture in cheese takes us from something like a soft, buttery and luscious, triple-cream Vignotte to crumbly Cheshire. Exploring textures in cheese, and learning to pair them so that every bite provides contrast, is a wonder in itself: the smoothness of a Vignotte can find harmony with the crunch of a toasted baguette or a slice of fresh apple. Finding contrast in textures needn't be complicated, and the results are always greater than the sum of their parts.

Intensity is measured by the hit of flavour (from bold and strong to gentle and mild) that each cheese gives on the palate. So, while a common feature of goat's cheeses is a sharp, citrus tang, the intensity of that tang can make or break a pairing. A pairing partner needs either to match the intensity of the cheese to create a harmony in the flavours of both, or to provide a delicate counterbalance that allows the cheese to shine.

The **finish** is the lasting impression a cheese leaves on your palate and reveals the cheese's depth and complexity. Think of finishes as ranging from smooth and mellow to sharp or even fiery. A pairing can enhance this experience, or smooth it out, depending on what you're looking for in the overall experience.

What makes a cheese *cheesy?*

Have you ever thought about why a Cheddar tastes like a Cheddar, which is so different from the flavour of a Stilton, which is completely different from a Camembert? Every one of these cheeses is cheesy in its own way, and yet you'd never confuse a burrata with an Edam or a Red Leicester with a soft goat's cheese. So, what are the influences that give each cheese its specific character, which make it an ideal pair for one particular cracker or another, or a certain chutney as opposed to a certain jam, or charcuterie as distinct from a piece of fruit?

In the world of cheese, possibilities are endless. Why? Because cheese is made from such a variety of milks, from animals that graze in fields from across the world, and because each of these fields has its own particular terroir – giving the animals' food source its own distinct characteristics. Cow's milk, ewe's milk, goat's milk, buffalo's milk, and even blends of milks – these distinct raw materials form the foundation of the unique personality in each cheese we want to pair.

But it's not just the milk and terroir that influence the cheesiness of a cheese. Seasonality plays a vital role, too. Livestock that graze on fresh grasses and wildflowers during the spring and summer produce milk that has a lower fat content than that from hay-fed animals during the autumn and winter. In turn, the artisan cheesemaker adjusts their cheesemaking techniques to produce a cheese that reflects the time of year – spring and summer cheeses tend to be those with a lighter, fruitier texture and, for those made with cow's milk, often yellower in colour (thanks to the beta-carotenes in the grasses – the same nutrients that give our fruits and vegetables their hue); winter cheeses are denser and richer, and (in cow's-milk cheeses) paler, because the drying process removes much of the beta-carotene from the grass. The signature flavour of goat's milk is due to higher levels caprylic acid, which also leads to lower fat levels – and therefore year-round paler cheese. The point in the animals' lactation cycle that a farmer obtains the milk makes a difference, too. Just as

with humans, the composition of the mother's milk changes with the changing dietary needs of her growing baby.

Artisan cheese is exactly that – an art – and, like an artist, each cheesemaker uses their own techniques to shape the character of their work (in this case, cheese). Curdling methods, types of fermentation, and the addition of specific bacteria or moulds contribute to the diversity in flavours and textures. Decisions about ageing, another pivotal aspect, infuse cheese with myriad forms of depth and complexity over time.

Finally, believe it or not, you can influence a cheese's cheesiness, too! A cheesemonger will often tell you not to serve cheese directly from the fridge, because serving temperature can make a huge difference to the character and flavour accents on your palate. And, of course, what you pair your cheese with will help to balance, accentuate, or create certain profiles in your experience of it. When you tuck in, remember that every bite tells you the story of the animals, terroir, season, production techniques, ageing, serving temperature and pairing of that cheese; every cheese tells a tale of nature, craftsmanship and the art of indulgence.

Over the following pages, I've put together a quick-reference guide to the main cheese characteristics and how each manifests in its main milk source, along with some examples of how you can sample those differences for yourself.

Fresh

Characteristics:
chalky • fluffy • moist • smooth • spreadable

The term 'fresh cheese' indicates that the milk has been curdled using a form of acid, often lemon juice or vinegar, and then the cheese, once it forms, is eaten before it ages and ripens. That's why fresh cheese is the baby among cheeses. Cow's milk fresh cheese tends to have a mild, dairy note and buttery flavour, while goat's milk gives tangy, salty and grassy flavours.

COW'S MILK
These cheeses are mild, milky and buttery
Burrata, cream cheese, Mascarpone, mozzarella, paneer, ricotta

GOAT'S MILK
These cheeses are mild, tangy, milky, floral and citrussy
Buchette, Cabécou, Chèvre

Brined Fresh

Characteristics:
moist • smooth • springy • squeaky • tender

Hard cheeses that have a short ageing period (which means they count as 'fresh'; see above) usually call for brining after pressing, which prevents a rind or mould forming around the cheese.

COW'S MILK
These cheeses are creamy, milky, salty and tangy
Cheese curds, queso fresco

EWE'S MILK
These cheeses are buttery, moist, savoury and sweet
Brebis (US-style), feta, Pecorino Sardo Dolce, ricotta

MIXED MILK
This cheese is creamy, rich and salty
Halloumi

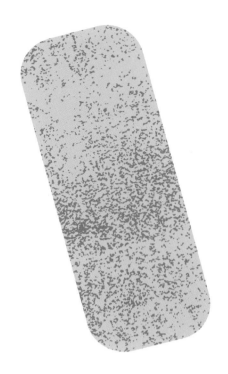

Bloomy

Characteristics:
creamy • delicate • mellow • milky • gooey • tangy

When soft cheeses mature they are covered with a white, downy rind. These rinds are made up of edible moulds, whichare often a mix of *Penicillium candidum* (fluffy white-coloured mould) and *Geotrichum candidum* (squiggly cream-coloured mould).

COW'S MILK
These cheeses are buttery, earthy, grassy, milky, mushroomy and rich
Brie, Camembert
Favourites: Baron Bigod, Brillat-Savarin, Coulommiers, Délice de Bourgogne, Tunworth, St Jude

GOAT'S MILK
These cheeses are buttery, grassy, herbaceous, tangy and salty
Ash-ripened goat's, goat's brie, soft-ripened goat's
Favourites: Chabis de Gâtine, Crottin de Chavignol, Garrotxa, Humboldt Fog, Selles-sur-Cher, Valençay

EWE'S MILK
These cheeses are buttery, nutty, milky and sweet
Brebirousse d'Argental, Little She, Pérail, Wigmore

Blue

Characteristics:
buttery • creamy • crumbly • soft • smooth

The veins in blue cheese are the result of a process that begins when cheesemakers introduce a live fungus to the milk or curds during the cheesemaking progress. Once the cheese is formed into rounds, the cheesemaker pokes small holes all over it (a process called 'needling') to create pockets of oxygen that allow the mould to multiply and spread for all that resulting deliciousness.

COW'S MILK
These cheeses are bold, peppery, pungent, tangy and tart
Bayley Hazen Blue, Bleu d'Auvergne, Cashel Blue, Cote Hill Blue, Gorgonzola, Fourme d'Ambert, Rouge River Blue, Shropshire Blue, Stichelton, Stilton

EWE'S MILK
These cheeses are rich, salty, spicy and sweet
Bleu des Causses, Crozier Blue, Roquefort, Valdeón

GOAT'S MILK
These cheeses are bold, herbaceous and tangy
Beacon Blue, Bleu de Chèvre, Cornish Nanny, Harbourne Blue

Washed Rind

Characteristics:
pungent • soft • sweet • supple • sticky • dense

In a washed rind cheese, the exterior of the cheese is washed with a brine that may be blended with beer, brandy, wine, cider or even Champagne to lend the cheese its distinct characteristics. The washing attracts salt-loving bacteria called 'haleophiles', which in turn give the cheese a noticeably deeper yellow or orange appearance and a pungent aroma.

COW'S MILK
These cheeses are smoky, meaty and pungent
Époisses, Langres, Livarot, Mont D'or, Munster, Pont-l'Évêque, Reblochon, Rollright, Stinking Bishop, Taleggio

EWE'S MILK
These cheeses are tangy, robust and rich
Riseley, St James, Quintano

GOAT'S MILK
These cheeses are full flavoured and funky
Apatha, Musgo Lavado, Rachel

Semi Hard

Characteristics:
shiny • smooth • supple • thick • waxy

With a slightly higher moisture content that gives a bouncier texture in the finished result than a fully hard cheese, semi-hard cheeses will hold their form when you cut a slice from them.

COW'S MILK
These cheeses are buttery, creamy, fruity, earthy, melt-in-the-mouth and nutty
Edam, Emmental, Fontina, young Gouda, Morbier, Raclette, Saint-Nectaire, Scamorza

GOAT'S MILK
These cheeses are gentle, tangy and smooth
Tomme de Chèvre, goat Gouda, Pico, Garrotxa, Caprino Romano

EWE'S MILK
These cheeses are milky, tangy, tart and slightly sweet
Abbaye de Belloc, Berkswell, young Manchego, Ossau-Iraty, young Pecorino

Hard

Characteristics:
crumbly • dense • rustic • thick

Hard cheeses owe their firmness to a combination of factors, including lower moisture content from pressing, longer ageing periods, lactic acid conversion during cheesemaking, and the aggregation of proteins and fats. These processes work together to create cheeses with dense, solid textures and distinct flavours that are characteristic of hard cheeses.

COW'S MILK
These cheeses are bold, nutty, piquant, sharp and strong
Beaufort, Caerphilly, aged Cheddar, Comté, mature Gouda, Gruyère, Lincolnshire Poacher, Mimolette, Parmigiano-Reggiano

GOAT'S MILK
These cheeses are rich, savoury, tangy and caramelly
Aged goat's Cheddar, goat's Gouda, Pantysgawn, Picodon

EWE'S MILK
These cheeses are savoury, sharp, slightly sweet and zesty
Abbaye de Belloc, aged Ossau-Iraty, Manchego, Pecorino

How do we taste?

Our experience of food is more than just the taste of it on our tongue – appreciating flavour involves a complex interplay of taste, aroma, texture and temperature; it's a sensory journey.

There are five basic tastes: sweet, salty, bitter, sour and umami and these are the tastes that we pick up via our taste buds. It seems inconceivable, but without anything else at play, that's it. These fundamental taste sensations helped our ancient selves make on-the-spot decisions about the food in front of us – they meant the difference between a full belly and a bellyache! When it comes to tasting cheese all these thousands of years later, we've got a special name for those five basic tastes – we call them the 'Simple Flavours' and they help us decide whether that cheese is a 'Yum, let's have more!' or a 'Hmm, maybe I'll pass on that one thanks.' When we enjoy a particular style of cheese, it's not because it tastes salty and nothing more; it's because of the intricate layers of flavour that develop way past that initial bite. How?

The notion that a cheese such as a Pecorino could have almond notes comes from our experience of flavour, which has a lot to do with our sense of smell. While our taste buds tell us the basic nature of what's on our tongue, the olfactory nerves that sit at the back of our throat and in our nose allow the flavour to bloom; our sense of smell adds depth and complexity to the overall experience. Pecorino is salty, but hold it on your tongue for a moment or two to break down and give your sense of smell a chance to focus, and the almondy notes will come through. It's alchemy! I would say that half of my customers come in to the shop because they smell all that deliciousness as they (attempt to) pass – they are already discerning the flavour of what they'll buy, long before I give them a sample to taste.

And then there's texture. Eating a soft and tangy cheese is a completely different gustatory encounter to sampling a hard and tangy one. A velvety brie or a creamy goat's cheese offers a different tactile sensation to a crumbly, aged Cheddar. The mouthfeel of a cheese influences our overall perception of flavour.

The temperature of your food has impact, too. Temperature can subtly alter the flavour profile, to intensify or mask certain layers of experience. For example, a room-temperature Camembert tastes more mushroomy and earthy than one that comes oozing from the oven. Equally, if you ate it straight from the fridge (which I wouldn't recommend), you'd find a cheese that's more lacklustre, without many of the subtleties of flavour and intended texture. With this in mind, always allow your cheeses to sit for 1–2 hours at room temperature before you eat them (unless you're baking, of course) to experience them at their very best. And take your time! A full flavour experience develops.

Find your *inner* fromager

If you're anything like me, being presented with a plate of delicious cheeses is simply an invitation to dive in, no questions asked. However, it's time to hold back: learning how to taste cheese properly, so that you can decipher all the layers that make it taste so good, will help you make great choices when it comes to pairing. Mastering the art of tasting cheese in a structured way gives you a deeper appreciation of the cheese and a confident understanding of what other morsel of deliciousness might best go with it. The following steps are your guide to tasting cheese (it's like wine tasting, but you can still drive afterwards).

1: Be prepared

First and foremost, if you're tasting more than one cheese in a sitting, choose a variety of cheeses (such as aged, soft, hard, blue-veined, and so on) that are of different strengths, and organize them for tasting mildest and lightest to strongest and most intense. This will help you to distinguish the subtle flavours in the mildest cheeses without your palate being overpowered by the cheese before. Don't choose too many cheeses, though – five is plenty if you're starting out on your tasting journey.

For similar reasons, don't consume any strong-tasting foods or drinks immediately before you taste – you want as neutral a palate as possible. It's good to have a glass of water and some neutral-flavoured biscuits on hand to clean your palate between cheeses if you're tasting more than one. Apple slices are also good for this purpose – they contain malic acid, which is a palate-cleanser. Use a clean plate, and an individual cheese knife for each cheese you intend to taste. Leave the cheeses to reach room temperature before you begin. If you're a cheese aficionado, you know better than to devour it straight out of the fridge! Cold cheese can be lacklustre, dry, crumbly and even rubbery.

Notes are crucial to refer back to, so make sure you have a notebook and pen ready.

2: Start with your eyes

Note down the cheese's colour, texture and any distinctive features, such as a downy layer on the rind or marbling on the cheese flesh. For example, some cheeses have what pros call an 'inorganic outer', which means the cheese is covered in wax, plasticoat or cloth. On the other hand, an 'organic outer' may refer to rinds made of charcoal, leaves or grape must. What colour is the rind, if there is one? And what colour is the interior (known as the 'paste') of the cheese – try to be specific: 'white' will prove a bit meaningless once you are several cheeses in, so try to find comparisons in nature or other parts of life to get really down to the nitty gritty – creamy white, daisy white or unbleached white will give you a better sense of what you mean. Is there a fleck of another colour? Are there holes in the cheese? Are they large or small? Again, be specific. All these initial, visual assessments can provide insights into the cheese's age, ripeness and craftsmanship.

3: Engage your sense of smell

Give the cheese a good sniff. First, assess the intensity of the smell by holding the cheese at arm's length and bringing it closer to your nose – the closer you get it before you can smell it, the lower the intensity. Next, identify the presence of ammonia by smelling the rind (not the paste) – a strong ammonia smell might suggest the cheese is overripe. Then, explore other aromas in the cheese as a whole. Does it have a strong dairy smell? If so, does it smell like cow's milk, goat's milk or ewe's? Is the cheese fruity, floral or leafy, vegetable, mineral, or chemical? In all cases, take time to be as specific as you can – which fruits, flowers, vegetables, minerals or chemicals come to mind? (It's also worth saying at this point that there are no rights and wrongs – you're trying to establish a profile that will enable you to pair your cheese well, so if you smell something like old boots or wet fur, say so!)

4: Feel it in your fingers

Use your sense of touch to inspect the cheese – feel its texture between your fingers. The texture of the paste could range from soft (think, fresh goat's curd) to hard (an aged Gouda). The consistency could be crystalline (think, Parmesan) or crumbly (Wensleydale). Again, try to be specific and draw comparisons with other familiar items or foods or the natural world. Note the cheese's density (is it porous or solid; rubbery or stiff), moisture content (does it feel at all wet or oily, or is it totally dry between your fingers?), and any other unique touch characteristics.

5: Take a small bite

I know you've been really patient so far, but I implore you to hold back a little longer. Rest the small bite of cheese on your tongue for just a few seconds – this will get your saliva working, which will help to break down the cheese and release all those yummy aromas. Then, slowly chew the cheese, giving all the smell receptors at the back of your throat an opportunity to find flavour from within. Pay attention to the initial taste, and then consider how that evolves as you chew. Which of the five basic tastes does it begin as (see page 16). Then, as the flavour develops, think about the complexities. Start broad (look, for example, for nutty, earthy, dairy, fruity, fresh, zesty). Then, with each moment try to drill down to make your observations more specific. Make notes as you go – the evolution of the flavour is as important as the end result.

6: Analyze the finish

Now swallow. What is the residual flavour left on your tongue? Does it linger or does it dissipate quickly? As you might expect, stronger cheeses tend to have a long finish. If it lingers, does the flavour change as it loses its intensity? Take a moment to reflect on your overall impression of the cheese. Compare it to other cheeses you've tasted – what are its similarities and in what ways is it unique? Can you immediately think of any other food or drink that might go well with it? You'll find my top tips for pairing over the page.

Pair like a *pro*

In the world of cheese pairing, achieving the perfect match isn't just a matter of chance. It's an art that revolves around three key principles: enhancing, balancing and contrasting. Here's how these principles shape our cheese-pairing experiences.

Enhance: flavour and texture

When we choose a pairing that enhances, we're essentially using another element (a food or drink, perhaps) to magnify the cheese's unique characteristics. Enhancing excites both our taste buds and our other sensory perception. Consider how pecans bring out the nutty undertones of a mature Cheddar – the nuts are there to highlight their own characteristic in the cheese. But it's not just flavour that we can enhance – texture works this way, too. Imagine the the firm edge of a grape that gives way to a soft inside, and pair that with a velvety Camembert with its bloomy rind.

Balance: finding equilibrium

Balancing is all about considering a cheese's intensity and finding a pair that brings equilibrium. For example, when enjoying a pungent blue cheese, the sweetness of ripe pear alongside can tame its boldness. Furthermore, we can look for all-round balance in the five basic tastes (see page 16) – if the cheese brings salty and sweet, we might want to find a pair that brings umami, sourness and/or bitterness, too.

Contrast: exploring diversity

As the name suggests, contrast in a cheese pairing is about embracing diversity in flavours and textures. Imagine a piece of sharp goat's cheese paired with a square of milk chocolate. The sharpness of the cheese side by side with the sweet, milky chocolate creates layers of flavour explosion on the taste buds – a bit like a firework that keeps on giving. Contrasting texture, such as pairing crunchy crackers with a creamy Camembert, is another way we can use contrast to elevate the taste experience.

In the world of cheese pairing, the artistry lies not just in mastering one of these principles but in orchestrating a symphony of effects. A well-crafted pairing can simultaneously enhance flavour, balance intensity, and provide a delightful contrast in texture. It's the ultimate aim for cheese connoisseurs like me to combine many of these effects in a single pairing. Sometimes, we can make those effects even more stunning by using a 'bridge'.

When a pair becomes a threesome

A 'bridge' is a third element in a cheese pair. For example, think about a Pecorino Toscano, red Sangiovese wine and cherry jam (see page 101). The jam is the bridge between the soft fruitiness in the wine and the orchard, earthy intensity in the cheese. The result is to add complexity and depth to the pairing experience. Whether it's another food, a drink or a unique condiment, embracing a threesome opens up a world of flavour sensation.

Steps to pairing

Before you begin your own pairing journey, organize a little test tasting with a friend – the first part of this process echoes the steps we looked at on pages 18–19. This time, though, we're going to take it further and use what we learn to find some good pairs.

Pick no more than five cheeses to start with, each of a different variety. For example, you might choose a blue-veined cheese such as Roquefort or Stilton, a soft cheese such as a mild Camembert or brie, an aged cheese, such as a mature Cheddar or Parmesan, and so on. Beginning with the mildest cheese in your selection, pick up a small piece (not more than a small mouthful-size). First, take a good look at the cheese and note down everything you see about it's colour, appearance and even texture. What clues might it give you about its flavour? Next, close your eyes and smell the cheese. Give it a good sniff, then open your eyes and note down what the smell reminds you of – draw comparisons with other familiar smells to try to be as specific as you can. For example, don't conclude just 'sweet', but be more detailed – do you mean sweet like pineapple or like candyfloss, for example? Like sweet tea or like a boiled sweet? Next, pop the piece of cheese into your mouth and let it rest on your tongue.

Leave the flavours to soak in – again, it might help to close your eyes so you can really focus. Then, note down everything you can about its taste, flavour and texture. Be specific, just as you were with the aroma, and consider how flavour and texture might change over the course of chewing the cheese. Finally, swallow. What are the after-effects on your tongue? Is there a lingering finish? Note it down.

Now, look at your notes and think of flavours, aromas and textures that could balance, contrast and enhance the flavours, aromas and textures you identified in the cheese. Think about each of these categories in terms of which complement and which contradict. Make a list summarizing the flavours or characteristics you might look for in an accompaniment for the cheese. Now consider what foods and drinks fulfil some, most or all of those characteristics (think as broadly or as specifically as you like – flavoured chocolate or crackers, or cocktails, as well as fruits and vegetables, say, just as they come). Remember to think about texture and mouthfeel as well as flavour and aroma – creating a great pairing is a whole-sense experience.

This is the detail a cheese pro will use when tasting cheeses. Always keep a note of what works and what doesn't – your own reference book will have you pairing like a pro before you know it!

How to use the charts

So, here it is: the reason why we're here – my cheese-pairing charts and curated boards. Over the following pages, I've created 24 pairing boards to help you get started on your own pairing journey. Each section in this chapter focuses on a main pairing category – food, drink, seasons and around the world.

Within each section are the boards, each zooming in on one particular category type, time or place. For example, Cheese & Foods has boards based around fruit, vegetables, charcuterie, crackers, nuts and much more. Drinks covers everything from wine through cocktails to tea and coffee. World introduces some lesser known pairings from cheese producing nations, alongside some familiar classic combinations. Seasons... well, takes each season in turn, celebrating the best produce available throughout the year. Following each pairing board are between one and three recipes, either to help you use the pairing in your cooking, as well as on a board, or to make your own perfect accompaniment.

For each board, the pairings appear both on the photograph, to give you a sense of how to design your board (remembering that tasting starts with the eyes!), and then pair-by-pair in the text, to give you brief flavour descriptions not only of the cheeses themselves but also what it is about them and their pair that works so well together. In each case, I've covered the principles of enhancing, contrasting and balancing the pairing experience (looking variously at aroma, texture and flavour), and for some boards, I've also suggested a bridge – that third element that helps to connect the pair together (see page 20).

Now, I know that not everyone has access to the kinds of artisan cheeses that I do (not a day goes by when I don't pinch myself for how lucky I am). So, all of these boards and pairings will work with widely available versions of the cheeses in question, as well as the specialist versions. I just urge you always to buy the best-quality you can. If you do have access to a fromagerie or cheesemonger in your neighbourhood, I've also given each pairing my 'favourite' – the speciality or artisan cheese that I think works best with the pair I've chosen. But, I want to stress, these are wishlist cheeses – don't feel constrained by them.

Each cheese is listed with its main milk-source provenance, but remember that some cheeses may be made with a variety of milks, or sometimes with cow's and other times with ewe's, for example, so the listings aren't hard-and-fast – do check the packaging if you want a particular style. Alongside, I have listed its intensity – the strength you're looking for in that cheese for this pairing. Intensity is measured on a scale from 1 (young, very mild cheeses) to 5 (strong, pungent and extra-mature cheeses). A single cheese may be marketed at various times in its ageing, and this can make a big difference to its intensity and flavour, so do check that number before you buy.

Finally, no matter how you arrange your board, don't forget to label your cheeses on there and include the intensities on your labels – so that you and your guests can enjoy them from mildest to strongest (see page 18) to get the best tasting experience possible. Let the fun begin!

CHEESE
PAIRING
CHARTS

The cheeses and pairings on this board represent my absolute go-tos – these are the pairings I know will impress and that are easy to get hold of, either in your local supermarket or a fromagerie. I've given you my favourite cheese for each pairing, but don't let that hold you back. The beauty of this board is that the pairings work with pretty much any producer of each cheese type, although (if you can) opt for artisan over commercially produced cheeses. These pairings are versatile and delicious all in one.

My favourites

BLUE CHEESE & OATCAKES with walnuts
• *Cow's milk* • *Colston Bassett Stilton* • *3*

Enhance Blue cheese and crackers – a classic! The creamy nature of a good blue cheese (Colston Bassett Stilton is my favourite and it's melt-in-the-mouth when it's at its peak) is given a starring role against the backdrop of the simple crackers, which do everything to allow the cheese to shine. But that's also not to forget the nuttiness in each of them – which makes for a gorgeous harmony.
Contrast Bold, spicy and pungent cheese flavours provide a strong contrast with the neutral flavours of the crackers. This is a dynamic, intense pairing.
Balance Creamy is balanced with crunchy; tangy is balanced with earthy; pungent is balanced with mild. Everything about this pairing is balance!
Bridge Both blue cheese and crackers have an underlying nuttiness that finds the ultimate bridge in walnuts. There's a creaminess to walnuts, too, which brings out the creaminess in both components of the pairing.

BRIE & BAGUETTE with dessert pear
• *Cow's milk* • *Brie de Meaux Dongé* • *3*

Enhance Who doesn't love to smother pillows of simple, sweet baguette with buttery, luscious brie? Simple, elegant luxury is everything when it comes to what's enhanced in this pairing.
Contrast A good baguette has a crisp, crunchy crust that is in direct contrast to the smooth, oozy nature of the brie.
Balance Flavour is where we find balance in this pairing. The creamy, mild sweetness of brie is balanced in the neutral, easygoing flavour of the baguette.
Bridge Choose a just-ripe dessert pear for your bridge here – you want a little bit of crunch left in the fruit to temper the sweetness. This helps to bridge the crunchy crust of the baguette with the creaminess of the brie, while the delicately floral sweetness brings out the sweetness in both bread and cheese.

COMTÉ & WHEAT CRACKERS
with dried apricots
• Cow's milk • Comté AOP Fort Saint Antoine • 3

Enhance Comté develops a layer of dark earthiness in its flavour thanks to its distinct provenance on the Massif in eastern France, where cows graze on Alpine pasture. Their milk is notably layered in flavour, which itself is intensified in the ageing process of the cheese – in the humid, cool caves beneath the hills. It's this complexity that is enhanced by pairing the cheese with a simple wheat cracker – nothing to overpower and everything to gain.

Contrast Comté is a good melting cheese, which gives a clue to its smooth, plump texture – contrast this with a crisp, crunchy cracker and you have an irresistibly moreish combination.

Balance Comté is a cheese with in-built balance – it is nutty, fresh and savoury at first bite, with a salty and very slightly sweet aftertaste. With a bitter cracker to finish off the experience, we have achieved greatness.

Bridge Dried apricots bring out the fruit sweetness and tangy side of the cheese, while the slight crunch as you bite into one makes for a good link between the smooth, firm cheese and the snap of the cracker.

MANCHEGO & RYE CRACKERS
with membrillo
• Ewe's milk • Queso Manchego • 3

Enhance A classic *pinchos* (bar snack), these two work so well together because each brings out the nuttiness and earthy undertones in the other. The cheese is rich and the crackers are robust, making them a brilliantly matched pair.

Contrast I love the way the saltiness in the cheese is contrasted with the earthy flavour of the rye. There is good texture contrast here, too. Manchego is a smooth, silky cheese, whereas rye crackers have a characteristically grainy nature.

Balance Manchego gives us sweet, salty and a slightly sour tang, while rye brings bitterness. Nutty and earthy in abundance, both elements of the pair bring umami.

Bridge Its sweetness, fragrance and slightly gritty texture make it no surprise that membrillo is the bridge for this classic pairing.

GOAT'S CHEESE & CHARCOAL CRACKERS
with fresh figs
• Goat's milk • Saint Maure de Touraine • 3

Enhance The delicate bitterness of the charcoal crackers is the perfect way to enhance the earthy, nutty flavour of goat's cheese. My favourite in this case, the Saint Maure de Touraine, highlights this even more, as this particular cheese has an ash rind.

Contrast The contrast between the cheese's creamy tanginess and the crackers' unique, smoky character is fabulous. However, I think the best contrast here is one for the eyes – bright white goat's cheese against a dark, almost-black cracker makes for a striking, mouthwatering pairing on a board.

Balance The firm texture of a more matured goat's cheese gives way to luxurious creaminess on the tongue, which is balanced out by the firm snap of the cracker. There is deep savouriness in this pairing, but the sour, fruity notes in the cheese bring natural balance overall.

Bridge The deep, purple-black skin of fresh figs not only complement the colours on the board here, but also act as a subtle link between the zesty sweetness of the cheese and the bitter cracker.

CHEDDAR & FRUIT TOAST with red grapes
• Cow's milk • Montgomery Cheddar • 3

Enhance The umami is strong in a good, mature Cheddar (Montgomery is wrapped in muslin and aged on oak shelves to enhance its savouriness), so while sweetness in the toast brings contrast (see below), it's the grains that make the dough that help to bring out the nutty, earthiness.

Contrast Cheddar offers a sharp, savoury contrast to the sweetness of the fruit toast. Texture contrasts here, too – an aged Cheddar has a good crumble, whereas the toast is crunchy at first bite and soft and pillowy inside.

Balance So much balance and harmony here! Savoury cheese and sweet fruit; tangy and sharp in the Cheddar balanced by an earthy bitterness in the lingering effects of the bread.

Bridge Juicy fruit works so well – linking the textures and flavours in the cheese and bread. Fresh red grapes pick out the sweetness of the raisins in the fruit toast and, at the same time, the zinginess in the cheese.

Cheese *and* food pairing

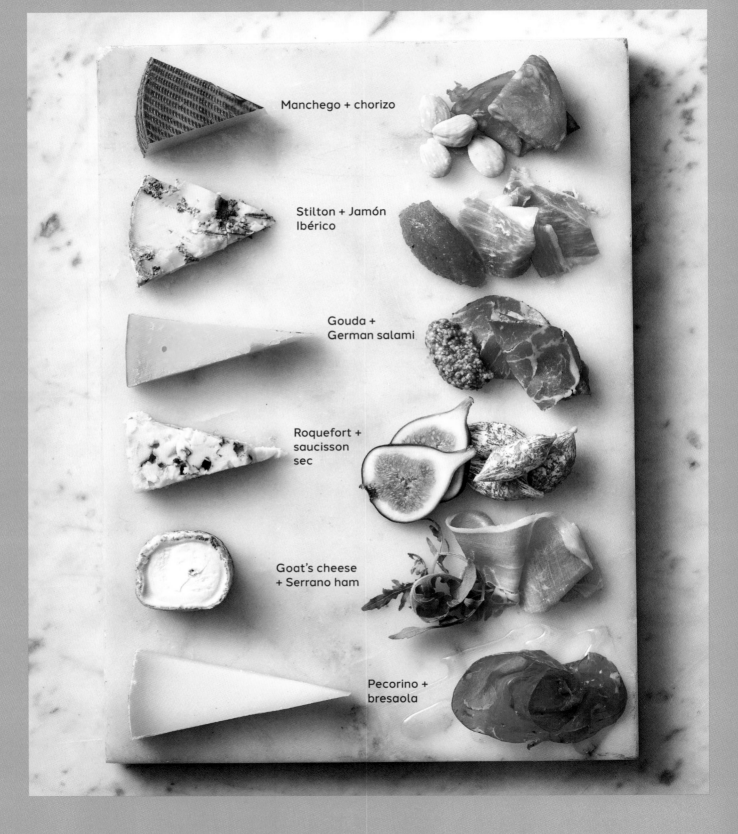

Manchego + chorizo

Stilton + Jamón
Ibérico

Gouda +
German salami

Roquefort +
saucisson
sec

Goat's cheese
+ Serrano ham

Pecorino +
bresaola

This board offers the ultimate in cured meats and cheese pairings. I'm featuring some old-time classics as well as breaking down borders to bring together some national cheese gems with charcuterie treats from other parts of the world. With the bridge flavours, too, this board would make a delicious lunchtime tasting experience.

Charcuterie

MANCHEGO & CHORIZO
with Marcona almonds
• *Ewe's milk* • *16 months mature* • *3*

Enhance Bold, spicy chorizo brings out the Manchego's nuttiness, which is what makes it a winner every time.
Contrast Manchego has a rounded creaminess that contrasts with the 'edginess' in the spice of the meat. Aged Manchego has had time to develop its sweetness, while the earthy meatiness in the sausage brings an underlying umami.
Balance Rich is balanced with bold when it comes to Manchego and chorizo, respectively.

STILTON & JAMÓN IBÉRICO
with membrillo
• *Cow's milk* • *Colston Bassett Stilton* • *4*

Enhance It would be easy to get lost in Stilton's strong, almost bitter flavour, but the silky, savoury notes of Jamón Ibérico help to remind us that even mature Stilton has an underlying creaminess.
Contrast The crumbliness of a mature Stilton contrasts beautifully with the delicate, melt-in-your-mouth texture of Jamón Ibérico.
Balance Mature Stilton will linger on the palate, the taste buds picking up its salty, bitter and sour notes. Jamón Ibérico brings heaps of deep umami, that 'fifth taste', to help provide balance.

GOUDA & GERMAN SALAMI
with wholegrain mustard
• *Cow's milk* • *Coolea* • *3*

Enhance Gouda and salami create a seamless fusion in which the savouriness of the salami enhances the cheese's mild sweetness.
Contrast I love the smooth texture of Gouda, which accompanies the slight grittiness in salami perfectly.
Balance In this pairing, the salami gives bold flavours, while the mild, sweet tones in the Gouda provide a foil.

ROQUEFORT & SAUCISSON SEC
with fresh figs
• *Ewe's milk* • *Roquefort Carles* • *4*

Enhance Despite its tanginess and strong flavour, Roquefort is creamy at its heart and the savouriness of the saucisson sec helps to bring out that gentle side.
Contrast Look for the herbal notes in the saucisson sec as they contrast with the sharp tang of Roquefort.
Balance Both flavours are rich and bold, but again it's the saucisson sec's deep herbiness that provides balance so that the Roquefort doesn't overpower.

GOAT'S CHEESE & SERRANO HAM
with rocket (arugula)
• *Goat's milk* • *Selles-sur-Cher and Blakesville Creamery Afterglow* • *2*

Enhance The rich and sour notes in goat's cheese come alive when paired with the savouriness of Serrano ham.
Contrast Serrano ham is aged and dried for long enough that it develops a deep, earthy flavour. This provides incredible contrast for the fresh goat's cheese.
Balance This pairing brings mild and delicate alongside bold and flavourful – the result is perfect.

PECORINO ROMANO & BRESAOLA
with lemon zest
• *Ewe's Milk* • *Pecorino Romano* • *3*

Enhance Bresaola (beef cured with herbs and spices) is deeply earthy and rich, which is exactly what the bold, salty tones of Pecorino Romano need to show themselves at their best.
Contrast Pecorino Romano is crumbly and flaky, which contrasts beautifully with the delicate, melt-in-your-mouth silkiness of bresaola.
Balance Robust flavours tempered with delicate; rough textures with smooth; salty and tangy with herbal and earthy – there is balance at every turn with this pairing.

Heaven-sent burrata, prosciutto & cherry tomato salad

The combination of creamy burrata, juicy tomatoes, tangy vinaigrette and salty prosciutto is definitely heaven-sent, arriving in your kitchen via the sunny climes of Italy. Burrata's velvety texture perfectly complements the sweetness of the tomatoes and the sharpness of the vinaigrette. Prosciutto brings a savoury element that enhances the umami of the tomatoes. This dish transports me straight to a Mediterranean paradise.

SERVES 1 AS A MAIN; 2 AS A SIDE

2–3 slices prosciutto, torn into small pieces

250g/9oz cherry tomatoes, halved

1 x 150g/5½oz ball of burrata

FOR THE DRESSING

1 tablespoon red wine vinegar

1 shallot, finely chopped

a small handful of flat-leaf parsley, leaves picked and chopped

¼ teaspoon flaked sea (kosher) salt

¼ teaspoon freshly ground black pepper

3 tablespoons extra-virgin olive oil

1 Preheat your oven to 190°C/170°C fan/375°F/Gas 5.

2 Arrange the torn prosciutto on a baking sheet and, once the oven is hot, bake it for 8–10 minutes, or until dark, golden and crispy.

3 While the prosciutto is crisping, in a small bowl, whisk together all the dressing ingredients until combined.

4 Tip the tomatoes into a bowl, pour in the dressing and toss the tomatoes until they are well coated. Transfer them to a serving platter, leaving any excess dressing in the bowl. Make a space in the middle of the tomatoes and place the ball of burrata into it.

5 Sprinkle the warm, crisp pieces of prosciutto all over the tomatoes and spoon over the dressing left in the bowl. Serve immediately.

Wine pairing: A light- to medium-bodied red wine, made from a grape such as Pinot Noir, or a Chianti, would be a great pairing for this heart-of-Italy salad. These wines have enough acidity and tannins to complement the richness of the burrata and prosciutto, while also standing up to the fresh sweetness of the cherry tomatoes.

Tortilla with vintage Manchego and chorizo

Straight from our charcuterie and cheese chart, this combo is as great in a Spanish omelette as it is on the board. It's delicious warm or cold, with a peppery rocket salad on the side.

SERVES 3–5

200g/7oz baby potatoes

2 tablespoons extra-virgin olive oil

1 large onion, finely sliced

1 teaspoon dried thyme, or picked leaves from 2 thyme (or rosemary) sprigs

6 eggs

50g/1¾oz Spanish (cured) chorizo, sliced into 5mm/¼in discs

2 handfuls of flat-leaf parsley, leaves picked and finely chopped

50g/1¾oz vintage Manchego, cut into a shavings with a knife or vegetable peeler, plus extra to serve

sea salt and freshly ground black pepper

rocket (arugula) salad, to serve

1 Bring a medium pan of salted water to the boil and add the potatoes. Boil for 7–10 minutes, until just tender (a little underdone is good), then drain them and when they are cool enough to handle, slice them in half. Set aside.

2 Heat the olive oil in a medium (about 24cm/9½in) deep, ovenproof frying pan or skillet over a medium heat. Add the onion and thyme and sauté for 7–10 minutes, until the onion is softened but not coloured.

3 While the onion is cooking, crack the eggs into a mixing bowl, season them with salt and pepper and whisk them until well combined. Set aside.

4 Add the chorizo to the onion in the frying pan and cook it for 5–8 minutes, or until it releases its oil. Tip the potatoes into the pan and stir them to coat them in the oil.

5 Heat the grill (broiler) to high.

6 Lower the heat, add the parsley and half the Manchego and pour in the eggs. Stir to distribute the ingredients throughout the egg mixture.

7 Cook the frittata in the pan for about 10–12 minutes, until the bottom has set and the top has almost set. Sprinkle over the remaining Manchego then transfer the pan to the grill and finish cooking the frittata until it's puffy and golden, and completely set.

8 Remove the frittata from the grill and leave it to rest in the pan for 5 minutes. Place a large chopping board on top of the pan and with one hand holding the pan and the other on the board, turn the tortilla out onto the chopping board. Sprinkle with Manchego, slice it into wedges and serve it with a rocket salad.

Parmesan + radiccio

Gouda + roasted carrots

Goat's cheese +
roasted beetroot

Fontina + sugar snap peas

Gorgonzola +
roasted cauliflower

Asiago + roasted
red peppers

Salad, root and green vegetables all feature in these pairings and some of them will need a bit of prep. The cheeses on this board, with the exception of the goat's, err on the side of strong, aged flavours, to ensure they are never overpowered by the flavourful veg.

Vegetables

PARMESAN & RADICCHIO
with balsamic glaze
• *Cow's milk* • *Parmigiano-Reggiano San Pietro* • *5*

Enhance The saltiness of the Parmesan is just what the bitter radicchio needs to show itself off, and vice versa.
Contrast I love the red–purple hue of radicchio leaves dotted with shavings of ochre-yellow Parmesan. The contrast between the crunch of the leaves and smooth, yet crumbly texture of the cheese never disappoints.
Balance Parmesan's nutty richness and deep umami are well balanced by the refreshing bitterness of radicchio. San Pietro Parmesan is a particularly fruity example of the cheese, which brings sweetness to the palate, too.

GOAT'S CHEESE & ROASTED BEETROOT
(**BEETS**) with candied pecans
• *Goat's milk* • *Luna Negra Raw Goat's* • *2*

Enhance Roasted beetroot retains the vegetable's earthy, autumnal quality, which is a great match for the mushroomy flavours in mild goat's cheese.
Contrast Goat's cheese brings a fresh tang that offsets the flavours and aroma of the beetroot beautifully. The caramelized sweetness from roasting provides contrast for the lingering acidity of the cheese.
Balance Creamy, decadent goat's cheese is balanced with the slight crunch of roasted beetroot.

GORGONZOLA & ROASTED
CAULIFLOWER with fresh thyme leaves
• *Cow's milk* • *Gorgonzola naturale* • *4*

Enhance The subtle flavours of cauliflower provide a sweetness to offset the cheese's tang and briny edge.
Contrast Roasted cauliflower provides a smoky, sweet flavour that contrasts beautifully with Gorgonzola's bold, spicy kick. Texture-wise, the rugged crunch of the cauliflower is a foil for the oozy, creamy cheese.
Balance Salt and sour in the cheese and sweet and bitter in the cauliflower, along with the umami of those gorgeous blue veins – all five tastes, right there!

FONTINA & SUGAR SNAP PEAS
with lemon zest
• *Cow's milk* • *Fontina Val d'Aosta DOP* • *4*

Enhance Aged Fontina has a subtle hint of roasted hazelnuts. The grassy, sweet notes of sugar snaps bring out the woodland flavours in the pairing.
Contrast I love the buttery texture of Fontina cheese – the crunch and fresh flavour of sugar snaps are perfect for making sure all that creaminess doesn't overwhelm.
Balance The aged Fontina provides a sour note that the natural sweetness in the fresh peas counteracts.

ASIAGO & ROASTED RED PEPPERS
with toasted pine nuts
• *Cow's milk* • *Asiago d'Allevo* • *5*

Enhance The earthy, toasted flavours of Asiago find harmony in the smokiness of the red peppers, while both have a sweetness that makes sure these two bring out the best in one another.
Contrast Roasted peppers bring sweet freshness, a contrast that makes sure the complexity of the cheese never overwhelms.
Balance An aged Asagio has a firm texture that balances the softness of the roasted peppers well.

GOUDA & ROASTED CARROTS
with honey
• *Cow's milk* • *Old Groendal* • *5*

Enhance Aged Gouda, or Gouda-style cheese, has an intense, roasted-almond character, which pairs well with root-vegetables. The sweet, caramelized roasted carrots complement the caramel notes in this cheese.
Contrast Crystallization in the cheese contrasts with the smooth, silky roast carrots. Leaving a texture at the centre of the carrots makes sure that the soft bite into the cheese is offset by a gently firm crunch.
Balance There's a lot of sweetness in this pairing, so to achieve balance on your palate focus on any sour and tangy notes characteristic of this cheese, too.

Fancy goat's curd canapés

These are the perfect canapé with the perfect cheese pairing. The earthy sweetness of roasted beetroot perfectly complements the creamy tanginess of goat's curd. Topped with fresh thyme leaves and drizzled with extra-virgin olive oil, these bite-sized delights are layered with flavour. Finishing them with homemade beetroot crisps not only adds a delightful crunch, but also makes them as stunning to look at as they are delicious to eat.

MAKES 20

2 beetroots (beets)

150g/5½oz goat's curd

extra-virgin olive oil, for drizzling

a few thyme sprigs, leaves picked

sea salt and freshly ground black pepper

FOR THE BEETROOT CRISPS

1 small beetroot (beet), peeled and thinly sliced

2 tablespoons olive oil

1 First, roast the beetroots. Preheat the oven to 200°C/180°C fan/400°F/ Gas 6. Cut off the tops of the beetroots, if they have them, then wrap each beetroot in foil and place them on a lipped roasting tray. Bake for 50–60 minutes, until the flesh is tender to the point of a sharp knife. Remove the beetroots from the oven and, when they are cool enough to handle, gently use a piece of kitchen paper to rub away the skin. Set aside.

2 To make the beetroot crisps, preheat your oven to 180°C/160°C fan/350°F/ Gas 4. Line a baking sheet with parchment paper.

3 Toss the thinly sliced beetroot in a bowl with the olive oil and a seasoning of sea salt. Arrange the slices in a single layer on the prepared baking sheet and bake them for 10–15 minutes, until the slices are crispy and slightly curled. Remove from the oven and set aside.

4 To assemble the canapés, cut the roasted beetroot into 2mm/^{1}/$_{16}$in slices. Top each slice with a small spoonful of goat's curd, then arrange the topped slices on a serving platter. Drizzle them with extra-virgin olive oil and sprinkle them with the fresh thyme leaves. Season with sea salt and black pepper. At this point you can cover the canapes and set aside, until you're ready to serve.

5 Just before serving, garnish each canapé with a beetroot crisp for added crunch and visual appeal.

Wine pairing: A dry rosé with fruity and floral notes would be a refreshing choice to balance the earthiness of the beetroot. Look for a rosé with good acidity, such as a Provençal rosé or a dry one from the Loire Valley. Alternatively, the herbaceous and citrussy characteristics of Sauvignon Blanc can complement the fresh thyme and goat's curd.

The best roasted carrots

This seasonal sensation is straight from the vegetable pairing board. This recipe elevates the humble carrot with a mouthwatering glaze, creamy yogurt sauce, nutty Gouda, fresh herbs, crunchy pistachios and vibrant pomegranate seeds.

SERVES 2–3 (AS A SIDE)

1 bunch of small carrots (about 300g/10½oz), green tops removed and reserved, and peeled

2 tablespoons chopped chives

2 tablespoons chopped dill

2 tablespoons chopped carrot tops

50g/1¾oz Gouda, finely grated

3 tablespoons chopped pistachios

2 tablespoons pomegranate seeds

FOR THE GLAZE

1 garlic clove, grated

zest of 1 unwaxed lemon

1 teaspoon smoked paprika

1 tablespoon pure maple syrup

a pinch of ground cinnamon

a pinch of ground cumin

3 tablespoons olive oil

sea salt and freshly ground black pepper

FOR THE CREAMY SAUCE

4 tablespoons full-fat Greek yogurt

1 tablespoon lemon juice

1 Preheat your oven to 220°C/200°C fan/425°F/Gas 7 and line a baking sheet with parchment paper.

2 Meanwhile, in a bowl, combine all the ingredients for the glaze and season it with salt and pepper.

3 Place the carrots on the lined baking sheet, and pour over the glaze, turning the carrots to coat them in the mixture. Transfer the baking sheet to the oven and roast the carrots for about 20–25 minutes, or until they are slightly caramelized.

4 While the carrots are roasting, prepare the creamy sauce. In a small bowl, mix the Greek yogurt with the lemon juice and season to taste. Set aside until the carrots are roasted.

5 Once the carrots are ready, transfer them to a serving dish. Drizzle them with the sauce and season with salt and pepper, then garnish with the chives, dill and carrot tops for a burst of freshness and colour. Sprinkle the grated Gouda and chopped pistachios on top, adding richness and a crunchy and nutty essence to the dish. Finish with a sprinkling of pomegranate seeds for a final burst of sweetness and vibrancy.

Baked artichokes with Pecorino

Known in Italy as *carciofi ripieni*, baked artichokes are a delicious and flavourful way to enjoy in-season artichokes with Pecorino Romano cheese. I remember my mother spending hours in the kitchen, carefully preparing the artichokes and stuffing them with mouthwatering ingredients. The preparation in this dish takes a while, but the end result is absolutely worth it – tender artichokes filled with the savoury goodness of melty cheese, garlic, parsley and breadcrumbs, all drizzled with olive oil. YUM!

SERVES 4

4 large artichokes

1 lemon, halved

110g/3¾oz dried breadcrumbs

130g/4½oz Pecorino Romano, grated

60g/2oz flat-leaf parsley, leaves picked and chopped

100g/3½oz Scamorza, shredded

4 garlic cloves, very finely chopped or grated

120ml/4fl oz olive oil

sea salt and freshly ground black pepper

1 Preheat your oven to 200°C/180°C fan/400°F/Gas 6.

2 Wash the artichokes thoroughly under running water; then remove the tough outer leaves and trim the stems. Cut off the top of each artichoke to remove the thorny tips of the remaining leaves. Using your hands or a spoon, gently spread the leaves apart, creating a cavity in the centre of the artichoke. You may need to use a knife to cut away some of the inner leaves to make room for the stuffing. To help prevent the artichoke from turning brown while you prepare the stuffing, you can rub the cut surfaces with a lemon half. (My mum bashes them against a hard surface to open them up slightly.)

3 In a large bowl, mix together the breadcrumbs, Pecorino, parsley, Scamorza and garlic, and season with salt and pepper to taste. Stuff the mixture between the leaves of each artichoke, pressing down firmly to pack it in.

4 Place the stuffed artichokes in a baking dish and drizzle the olive oil equally over the top of each. Pour about 250ml/9fl oz of water into the bottom of the dish, taking care to avoid getting any water on the stuffed artichokes themselves.

5 Cover the dish with foil and bake the artichokes for 45–50 minutes, or until the artichokes are tender – if you can pull a leaf out very easily, the artichoke is cooked. Remove the foil and bake for an additional 10 minutes, or until the stuffing is crispy and golden brown. Serve immediately.

Wine pairing: A crisp and refreshing white wine, such as a Pinot Grigio or Sauvignon Blanc is the ticket here. The acidity in the wine helps to cut through the richness of the cheese and complement the earthy flavour of the artichokes.

Cheddar + pineapple

Gorgonzola + papaya

Ricotta + strawberries

Goat's cheese + fresh figs

Parmesan + mango

Stichelton + dragonfruit

Gouda + blueberries

Feta + watermelon

Brie + white grapes

The tapestry of the world's fruit is an embarrassment of riches, and I'm hoping that by demonstrating how the underlying flavour profiles of each fruit work with different cheeses, you'll have the confidence to experiment with some alternatives of your own. This board could have become a book in itself!

Fruit

BRIE & WHITE GRAPES
• *Cow's milk* • *Somerset brie* • *2*

Enhance There's a tang to brie which is tempted out of the layers of buttery, rich flavour with a pairing of white grapes, which have a more sour taste than red or black.
Contrast Crunch and cream contrast in this pairing – the burst of crisp, fresh fruit mopping up all that decadent, sumptuous texture in the cheese.
Balance Earthy umami flows in abundance from a creamy, nutty brie, and it provides the backdrop to the sour and sweet grapes and bitter saltiness in the cheese.

RICOTTA & STRAWBERRIES
• *Ewe's milk* • *fresh ricotta* • *1*

Enhance Young ricotta is delicately sweet and this is brought to the fore by the strawberries. Both are fresh and lively, which makes them so moreish together.
Contrast The best strawberries have a natural sweetness that is offset by tart juice. Serve them and the cheese at room temperature, making sure that all those fruit layers come out to contrast with the creamy ricotta.
Balance Ricotta has a slightly tacky mouthfeel that is balanced by the smooth freshness of the strawberries.

GOUDA & BLUEBERRIES
• *Mixed milks* • *Semi-mature Cornish Gouda* • *3*

Enhance I'm focusing on Goudas that have a medium maturity, which holds their fudgy texture and butterscotch flavours. It's that relatively youthful nature that tart blueberries are so good at bringing to the fore.
Contrast Bite into a blueberry and a burst of sweet but tangy juice hits your palate – this makes the perfect contrast for the semi-firm fudginess in the Gouda.
Balance A sniff of a punnet of blueberries gives you their floral candy-sweetness. That's balanced perfectly by the umami-rich nuttiness of the cheese.

PARMESAN & MANGO
• *Cow's milk* • *Parmigiano San Pietro 25 months* • *5*

Enhance The Parmesan complements an underlying sour tang in a just-ripe mango; the mango complements the piney freshness in the cheese.
Contrast Savoury, Mediterranean aromas meet the heady sweetness of tropical fruit. This contrast brings sunshine from all horizons.
Balance Inviting the spicy notes of the Parmesan to balance the intense candy notes of the mango makes them a good match for each other.

CHEDDAR & PINEAPPLE
• *Cow's milk* • *Keen's or Fiscalini Farmstead* • *3*

Enhance Cheddar is known for its fruity undertones, a characteristic of a compound called ethyl hexanoate that is present in many strong-flavoured hard cheeses. The compound imparts a pineapple-like flavour – which makes pineapple itself perfect for picking it out.
Contrast The sweet hit of the pineapple gives way to a lingering salty savouriness in the cheese's finish.
Balance The butterscotch notes in the cheese and the zesty freshness of the pineapple lend exquisite balance.

GORGONZOLA & PAPAYA
• *Cow's milk* • *Gorgonzola Piaccante DOP* • *5*

Enhance This cheese has layers of spiciness and sourness but the papaya, with its soft, smooth flesh, is brilliant at reminding us to keep in mind the cheese's fundamental milky characteristic.
Contrast Gorgonzola piccante has deep-blue veins that are intensely aromatic, salty and sharp. What better contrast, then, than the gloriously juicy and sweet, orange flesh of a ripe papaya?
Balance Giving the papaya the job of bringing sweetness to the table, this pairing balances well the umami, sour and salty nature of Gorgonzola piccante.

Try also:
Feta & watermelon
Goat's cheese & fresh figs
Stichelton & dragonfruit

Baked Camembert with apricot

Creamy Camembert finds its perfect partner in the sweet, tangy apricot jam and dried apricots in this baked round. Nuts add crunch and chilli adds a hint of fire, offset with the sweetness of honey and zestiness of orange. It's a worthy twist on this classic sharing plate.

SERVES 2

1 round Camembert (250g/9oz)

2 tablespoons apricot jam

80g/2¾oz dried apricots, chopped

60g/2oz mixed nuts (such as almonds, walnuts and pistachios)

½–1 red chilli, deseeded and thinly sliced

2 tablespoons runny honey

finely grated zest of 1 orange, plus an optional squeeze of juice

a few thyme sprigs, to garnish

1 baguette, sliced, for dipping

1 Preheat your oven to 180°C/160°C fan/350°F/Gas 4.

2 Remove the Camembert from its packaging and place it in a small, ovenproof dish. Score the top of the Camembert with a sharp knife in a criss-cross pattern to allow the toppings to seep in when baking. Set aside.

3 In a small bowl, combine the jam, chopped dried apricots, mixed nuts, and half of the sliced chilli. Drizzle the honey over the apricot and nut mixture, then spoon the mixture over the scored Camembert.

4 If you like your food spicy, scatter the remaining half of the sliced chilli over the top. Finally, sprinkle over the grated orange zest. Place the Camembert in the oven and bake it for about 10–12 minutes, or until the cheese is soft and bubbling.

5 Remove the Camembert from the oven. I like to squeeze a little fresh orange juice over the top for an extra burst of citrus. Scatter with the thyme sprigs; then serve with the baguette slices for dipping.

Baked feta filo with watermelon

The combination of these ingredients in a neat parcel brings rich, crisp and sweet, all elevated by the invigorating flavours of mint and juicy watermelon to enjoy on the side. This sensational dish will transport you to the sun-kissed shores of Greece.

SERVES 2

250g/9oz block of feta

4 sheets of filo (phyllo) pastry

100g/3½oz unsalted butter, melted

2 tablespoons runny honey

a few mint leaves, to garnish

a few slices of watermelon, to serve

1 Preheat the oven to 180°C/160°C fan/350°F/Gas 4 and line a baking sheet with parchment paper.

2 Carefully unwrap the filo pastry sheets and cover them with a damp cloth to prevent them drying out.

3 Take one sheet of filo pastry and brush it lightly with some of the melted butter. Place another sheet on top and repeat the process until you have four layers of filo, each brushed with melted butter.

4 Cut the layered filo sheets into a square that is slightly larger than the feta block. Place the feta in the centre of the filo square, then drizzle the honey over the cheese, allowing it to gently coat the surface. Fold the phyllo pastry over the feta, sealing it into a neat package. Brush the outside of the parcel with melted butter to enhance its golden crispiness.

5 Transfer the wrapped feta cheese to the prepared baking sheet and bake for approximately 15 minutes, or until the filo pastry turns golden brown and crispy. Remove the parcel from the oven and let it cool for a few minutes.

6 To serve, place the baked feta parcel on a platter adorned with fresh mint leaves. Accompany it with slices of juicy watermelon, enhancing the dish's vibrant flavours and providing a refreshing contrast.

Wensleydale + Lincolnshire plum bread

Brie + baguette

Cheddar + wholewheat sourdough

Parmesan + ciabatta

Goat's cheese + rosemary focaccia

Brie + croissant

Cream cheese + pumpernickel

Gouda + sourdough

Bakery treats come in so many guises – from the irresistible crunch of a baguette to the tender flakiness of a croissant. This makes pairing cheese and bread (or other baked goods) a much more nuanced task than it might at first seem. And, if you're me, experimenting and finding the perfect match is the best way to spend an afternoon.

Bakery

BRIE & BAGUETTE with red grapes
• *Cow's milk* • *Baron Bigod* • *3*

Enhance As timeless as pairings come, creamy, buttery brie melds seamlessly with the sweet simplicity of baguette – a canvas on which the brie can shine.
Contrast Focus on the texture here – oozy cheese and crusty bread. There's no better more satisfying contrast in any cheese experience!
Balance As artisan cheeses go, the way in which Baron Bigod is made ensures that there is the perfect balance of cultures on the rind as the cheese matures. In that way, this brie, particularly, has a harmonious complexity in its bitter, sour, salty and umami (particularly truffle and mushroom) flavours. Crunchy and pillowy baguette rounds off this whole experience.

GOUDA & SOURDOUGH
with caramelized onions
• *Cow's milk* • *Coolea* • *3*

Enhance Sourdough bread – made using a live starter of flour and water, rather than baker's yeast – is the ultimate rustic loaf to go with this farmhouse-style cheese, each enhancing the earthy qualities of the other.
Contrast Gouda is a rich, flavourful cheese, with a thick, hard wax rind that holds in and intensifies the cheese's characteristics. The result is a sweetness to the Gouda that is offset by the tanginess of the sourdough.
Balance Take a mouthful of the cheese, then a mouthful of the bread to balance the richness of flavour. Sweet and savoury are in perfect harmony in this pairing.

GOAT'S CHEESE & ROSEMARY FOCACCIA
with balsamic glaze
• *Goat's milk* • *Ticklemore* • *3*

Enhance The earthy, herb-infused notes of focaccia seamlessly complement the herbal notes in this goat's cheese. My favourite here, Ticklemore, is left to develop its own rind during ageing, which makes it especially earthy and fresh in flavour.
Contrast Focaccia typically has a chewy texture, which contrasts beautifully with the velvety, creamy mouthfeel of the soft goat's cheese.
Balance Salty cheese and sweet bread – each have their own lingering savouriness on the palate.

PARMESAN & CIABATTA with fresh basil
• *Cow's milk* • *Parmigiano-Reggiano* • *5*

Enhance I'm sticking with Italy here, so that these two can do what comes naturally to them – bring out the best in each other. Rustic, low-salt ciabatta is the best canvas to show off salty, savoury Parmigiano-Reggiano.
Contrast Ciabatta has a distinctive chew, as a result of its strong, aerated structure – in contrast to the crumbly, compact texture of extra-mature Parmesan.
Balance Aged Parmesan is so complex! Nutty, salty, savoury and almost spicy on the tongue, it is a feast for the senses. The gentle flavour of ciabatta, with its herbaceous notes of olive oil, counters all those fireworks seamlessly.

CHEDDAR & WHOLEWHEAT SOURDOUGH with wholegrain mustard
• *Cow's milk* • *Montgomery Cheddar* • *3*

Enhance Robust, homely wholewheat sourdough is the best backdrop to make the sharp zestiness of a mature Cheddar pop. Montgomery Cheddar is a particularly rich and flavourful example that is beautifully offset by this bread.
Contrast Texture contrast is strong here – chewy wholewheat sourdough against creamy Cheddar cheese – but I love the contrast in the aromas, too. Nutty, woody bread and piquant, spicy cheese. Heaven!
Balance Mature Cheddar is ripe with umami, which is balanced by a salty and sour edge. Hedgerow sweetness in the bread sings delicious harmony.

CREAM CHEESE & PUMPERNICKEL
with fresh dill
• *Cow's milk* • *Pavé D'Affinois* • *1*

Enhance Dark, rich and sweet, pumpernickel is a malty rye bread that gives the luxurious creaminess of the cheese the chance to show off. My favourite here, Pavé D'Affinois, is a double-cream cheese, making it especially rich and decadent on the bread.
Contrast There's a molasses-like chewiness in pumpernickel that's a great foil for velvety, gooey cream cheese. I also love the contrast between the earthiness of the bread and the pungency of the cheese.
Balance Pumpernickel manages to achieve sweet and sour on its own, so add the umami and salty flavour of the cream cheese and you have almost a full complement of essential tastes.

BRIE & CROISSANT with fig jam
• *Cow's milk* • *Brie de Meaux Dongé* • *3*

Enhance These two are in it together for the most decadent party of flavours and textures! Each of them brings a sense of luxury – buttery, flaky pastry layers and velvety, silky, rich brie. Wonderful!
Contrast The ultimate patisserie breakfast is reinvented here so that its sweetness is offset by the sharp flavours in the ripe brie. This is a pairing of perfect contrast for the palate.
Balance I've chosen Brie de Meaux Dongé for my favourite here because it carries a mushroomy, almondy aroma that becomes deep umami on the palate, then leaves a slightly sour and bitter hint on the tongue. The sweet croissant completes the flavour profile perfectly.

WENSLEYDALE & LINCOLNSHIRE PLUM BREAD with spiced apple chutney
• *Cow's milk* • *Yoredale* • *2*

Enhance Wensleydale cheese (called Yorkshire Wensleydale only if it's made there) is subtly floral, with grassy notes. Underlying that freshness, though, is a characteristic honey sweetness that is brought out by the sweet plum bread, studded as it is with dried fruit.
Contrast Dense and wholesome, the plum bread provides good texture contrast for creamy, but crumbly Wensleydale. If you choose my favourite, Yoredale, you'll find a smoothness that is a good contrast to the crumbly bread.
Balance There's a good balance between sweet and sour in this pairing – the acidity in the cheese gives those sharp topnotes, but the bread is ready with its sweet fruit to make sure they aren't overpowering.

Burrata crunchy croissant

Indulgent brunch incoming! This delectable dish combines the flaky goodness of a croissant with the creamy richness of burrata, the sweetness of honey and sugar, and the tanginess of balsamic vinegar. You'll never look back.

SERVES 2

2 large croissants

2 tablespoons light brown soft sugar

1 tablespoon runny honey

a knob of butter, melted

1 x 150g/5½oz ball of burrata

2 slices of honey roasted ham

2 small handfuls of rocket (arugula) leaves

a handful of shelled pistachios

balsamic vinegar, for drizzling

1 Use a rolling pin to gently flatten the croissants to about 5mm/¼in thick. In a small bowl, mix together the sugar and honey until well combined. Brush one side of each croissant with melted butter and drizzle with the sugar and honey mixture.

2 Heat a non-stick frying pan over medium heat. Place the croissants in the hot pan, brushed side down, and cook for 2–3 minutes, or until golden brown and crispy. Flip the croissants and cook for another 1–2 minutes, or until golden brown and crispy on both sides. Remove the croissants from the pan and let them cool for a few minutes, then slice them in half horizontally through the middle (to create a top and a bottom).

3 Cut the ball of burrata in half and scoop out the inside of each half with a spoon (you can use the 'shell' torn over pasta or in a salad). Spread the creamy middle evenly and equally over the cut side of the bottom half of each croissant. Top each with a slice of ham, a handful of rocket leaves, and a sprinkle of shelled pistachios, then drizzle with balsamic vinegar. Sandwich with the croissant tops and serve immediately.

Wine pairing: White wines made using the Pinot Grigio grape have a refreshing acidity and citrus notes that can complement the creamy richness of the burrata and the sweetness of honey.

Earl Grey Lincolnshire plum bread

This twist on a traditional tea loaf is a fusion of sweet, dried fruits (given the umbrella term 'plum' in days gone by) and aromatic Earl Grey (rather than regular) tea. Sweet, savoury and floral, it's a perfectly balanced loaf, with a moist texture, that is heavenly alongside a cheese platter.

MAKES 2 SMALL LOAVES

225g/8oz unsalted butter

340g/11¾oz caster (superfine) sugar

125g/4½oz currants

125g/4½oz raisins

125g/4½oz sultanas (golden raisins)

75g/2½oz dried mixed peel

250ml/9oz strong-brewed Earl Grey tea

450g/1lb self-raising flour

pinch of ground mixed spice

2 eggs, beaten

1 Preheat the oven to 140°C/120°C fan/275°F/Gas 1. Line 2 x 450g/1lb loaf tins with greased baking parchment.

2 Add the butter and sugar to a large saucepan and melt them together over a medium-low heat until the sugar has completely dissolved. Remove the pan from the heat and stir in the dried fruit, then pour over the tea. Give everything a stir and set aside to cool and infuse.

3 In a large bowl, combine the self-raising flour and pinch of mixed spice.

4 Add the cooled fruit mixture and the beaten eggs to the spiced flour, then fold them through until well combined so that the fruit is evenly distributed throughout.

5 Divide the batter between the prepared tins, then bake the loaves for about 60–70 minutes, or until a skewer inserted into the centre of each comes out clean. If the loaves aren't quite ready, bake for a further 10 minutes and test again. Remove the loaves from the oven and leave them to cool in the tins, then remove them and serve in slices. You can wrap a whole loaf tightly in cling film (plastic wrap) and store it in an airtight container for up to 5 days.

Cheddar +
Almonds

Gouda with
cumin + walnuts

Extra-mature
blue cheese +
pistachios

Tomme +
pecans

Camembert
+ hazelnuts

Goat's cheese
+ nut brittle

Nuts and cheese go together like honey and lemon, Fred and Ginger, Mickey and Minnie – which made this board both a delight and a heartbreak (what to leave out?!) to put together! I feel when it comes to pairing cheese and nuts, this is just the beginning...

Nuts

CHEDDAR & ALMONDS with fresh honey
• *Cow's milk* • *Keen's extra-mature* • 5

Enhance Keen's extra-mature Cheddar is worth the additional sixth-month wait for it to come to full flavour, and texture. The dense, moist texture gives a creaminess that almonds pick out superbly well.
Contrast Mild and subtle almonds are a great match to set off the full-bodied, oniony and salty aromas that are released as you chew on a fully matured Cheddar.
Balance Tangy citrus dominates in this powerful cheese so the gently sweet nuttiness of the almond brings good balance to round off a deeply complex and well-matched pairing.

GOUDA WITH CUMIN & WALNUTS with onion jam
• *Cow's milk* • *Leyden* • 3

Enhance The pleasing, springy texture of a Gouda is a clue to the creaminess of the paste on the palate. Walnuts have a butteriness that brings out those milk notes in the cheese.
Contrast Studded with cumin seeds, cumin-enriched Gouda brings warm spice to this cheeseboard. Fresh and lively among nuts, walnuts offset that spice.
Balance Walnuts, slightly bitter at first bite, giving way to light, sweet and grassy notes within, offer balance to the the aromatic spice in this cheese, itself tangy and tart. I just love the fulsomeness of this pairing!

EXTRA-MATURE BLUE CHEESE & PISTACHIOS with raspberry jam
• *Cow's milk* • *Jasper Hill Farm Bayley Hazen Blue* • 5

Enhance The initial lightly spicy (pepper more than chilli) notes of blue cheese yield to more herbaceous, forest-fresh flavours on the palate, which a fresh, grassy nut such as a pistachio is great at tempting to the fore.
Contrast I'm contrasting textures again here – young pistachios tend to have a softer texture than those that are aged, and that smooth crunch is so welcome against the intensely dense, creamy paste of this cheese.

Balance Stacks of umami in this pairing – there's a meatiness to an aged blue (which is why it's so good over griddled steak) that really packs that savoury punch. Nuts, too, are umami-rich, but also in this case bring sweetness, fresh-sour notes and that initial bitterness in the first bite. Perfect.

CAMEMBERT & HAZELNUTS with fresh pear
• *Cow's milk* • *Isigny Ste-Mère Raw Milk Camembert* • 5

Enhance I'm calling on hazelnuts here, as those chocolatey notes are dreamy alongside a rich and unctuous cheese, such as an aged Camembert.
Contrast Fruitiness is the best description of the aroma of a ripe camembert. The earthy, must-like aromas of hazelnuts are a complementary foil.
Balance Gooey and creamy Camembert is well balanced in hazelnuts, which have a sweet milkiness of their own, and a richness that lets the Camembert shine without letting it hog all the limelight.

GOAT'S CHEESE & NUT BRITTLE with micro greens
• *Ewe's milk* • *Dorstone* • 3

Enhance The subtle veining in Dorstone maintains a perfect equilibrium, avoiding overwhelming sourness or tartness. Paired with the intense sweetness of the nut brittle, it creates a fully rounded tasting experience.
Contrast Diverge Dorstone's fresh and citrussy flavour stands in striking contrast to the sweetness and caramelization of the nut brittle.
Balance The nut brittle provides a delightful crunch which cuts through the creamy and ice-cream-like Dorstone, creating a harmonious balance.

Try also:
Brie & walnuts
Tomme & pecans

Cashew nut brittle

This is an irresistible treat from my cheese and nut chart (see pages 60–61). There is good crunch from the cashews and sweet toffee, and a spicy kick in the hint of cayenne pepper, if you fancy it. I love the contrast of textures that brittle and creamy cheese bring to every bite.

MAKES 1 LARGE SLAB

125g/4½oz shelled cashews, roughly chopped

150g/5½oz granulated sugar

75g/2½oz unsalted butter

½ teaspoon fine sea salt

¼ teaspoon cayenne pepper (optional)

1 Line a baking sheet with baking parchment and set it aside.

2 Heat a dry frying pan over a medium heat and, when hot, tip in the chopped cashews. Toast the nuts, stirring occasionally, for 6–8 minutes, until they turn golden and fragrant. Remove the pan from the heat, tip the cashews out onto a plate (to stop them cooking) and set aside. If you prefer, you can roast the nuts in the oven. Scatter them over a baking sheet and roast them at 180°C/160°C fan/350°F/Gas 4 for 8–10 minutes, until golden – it takes a little longer and uses more energy, but the colour is generally more even.

3 Meanwhile, combine the sugar, butter, salt, cayenne, if using, and 75ml/2¼fl oz water in a small saucepan over a medium-low heat. Once the sugar has dissolved, turn the heat up and bring the mixture to a gentle simmer. Simmer for 15–20 minutes, or until the mixture has turned deep golden in colour.

4 Add the roasted cashews to the caramel mixture and stir well to combine, ensuring that all the nuts are coated with the caramel.

5 Pour the hot cashew brittle mixture onto a parchment-lined baking sheet, spreading it out with a spatula to create an even layer. Let the cashew brittle cool completely at room temperature until it hardens and becomes firm. Once cooled and hardened, break the brittle into small, bite-sized pieces. It will keep in an airtight jar for up to 14 days.

Brie + pickled pearl
onions

Cheddar + sweet
& spicy pickles

Gorgonzola dolce +
pickled radishes

Blue cheese +
pickled red
onions

Swiss cheese +
pickled cauliflower

Feta + kalamata
olives

Cheddar +
pickled carrots

So many cheeses give a salty tang, which means that the vinegary hit of pickles and the brininess of olives are natural accompaniments on a cheeseboard.

However, with this board I'm getting more specific – so that you can elevate this classic pairing to really set your taste buds alight.

Pickles + olives

FETA & KALAMATA OLIVES
with fresh oregano leaves
• *Goat's and/or ewe's milk • Odysea Organic • 1*

Enhance This is a deeply moreish combo with the feta and olives bringing out the saltiness in each other.
Contrast Creamy crumbliness and smooth creaminess offer texture contrast in this pairing. There's also mild flavour in this cheese that offers a contrast to the strong-tasting Kalamata olives.
Balance The hot, sunny climate and the mountainous terrain where the sheep and goats graze and the olives grow lead to a unique blend of flora in the animals' diet and nutrients for the olive groves, and perfect synergy on our palate.

BLUE CHEESE & PICKLED RED ONIONS
with candied pecans
• *Cow's milk • Shropshire Blue • 3*

Enhance This is a confident blue cheese to match and lift the bold, tangy flavour in the pickles.
Contrast I love the contrast of both flavour and texture here. Blue cheese is so intensely creamy in texture and rich in flavour and is beautifully offset by the crunch of the onions and their mouth-puckering taste.
Balance The balance in this pairing comes from their contrast – it's like a see-saw of flavour that swings between tart and tangy and bold and earthy.

CHEDDAR & PICKLED CARROTS
with toasted walnuts
• *Cow's milk • Isle of Mull Cheddar • 3*

Enhance The cows that produce the milk for Isle of Mull Cheddar are uniquely fed on the leftover grains from the mash that makes a local whisky. This gives the Cheddar a distinctively fruity, heady lilt that is brought to the fore by the tangy carrots.
Contrast As Cheddars go, this one is a little softer in texture than many others – the crunchy pickled carrots are a perfect foil.

Balance Deep, earthy and savoury, the umami in this cheese is balanced in the sweet and sour of the pickles.

SWISS CHEESE & PICKLED CAULIFLOWER with roasted red peppers
• *Cow's milk • Alp Blossom • 3*

Enhance Cauliflower is a vegetable that takes on the flavours of everything around it. Here, the pickled cauli is careful to draw out the mild mustard in the Swiss cheese, rather than overpower it.
Contrast If you can find Alp Blossom, please go for it – it's such an aromatic cheese with a rind embedded with herbs and flowers. The pickled cauliflower's sharp acidity makes the contrast a delight for the taste buds.
Balance Creamy, mild and sweet, Swiss cheese is looking for a balance that is sour and punchy. There's a softness to the texture of the cheese that is well balanced by cauliflower's gentler crunch.

GORGONZOLA DOLCE & PICKLED RADISHES with rocket (arugula)
• *Cow's milk • Gorgonzola al Cucchiaio • 3*

Enhance The bold, tangy flavour of Gorgonzola is enhanced by the pepperiness of pickled radishes. Gorgonzola al Cucchiaio offers a sweeter blue-cheese lift for the zesty and slightly spicy pickled radishes.
Contrast The crunch of a radish is all the contrast the palate needs when paired with this oozy, creamy texture of this decadent favourite cheese.
Balance This pairing achieves balance by merging the creaminess and tanginess of the Gorgonzola with acidity and spiciness in the pickled radishes.

Try also:
Brie & pickled pearl onions with buckwheat honey
Cheddar & sweet & spicy pickles with crusty wholegrain bread
Goat's cheese & pickled raspberries with sweet oat biscuits

Easy assorted pickles

Pickles and cheese are a classic combination – bringing tart, vinegary crunch to the creamy indulgence of some of our well-known favourites. I love the first combo of fennel, garlic and spices – the slightly numbing aniseed tang of fennel pairs perfectly with Munster, Langres and Raclette, in particular. If you aren't a fan of fennel, the pickled carrots or cauliflower make excellent alternatives.

Pickled fennel

MAKES 1 X 500ML/17FL OZ JAR

2 fennel bulbs, finely sliced lengthways

1 tablespoon fine sea salt, plus 2 teaspoons for salting the fennel

250ml/9fl oz white wine vinegar

2 tablespoons granulated sugar

1 teaspoon mustard seeds

1 teaspoon fennel seeds

½ teaspoon black peppercorns

peel strips from ½ orange

6 thyme sprigs

a small handful of flat-leaf parsley (about 6 stalks)

1 Add the fennel slices to a large bowl or dish. Pour over 500ml/17fl oz of water and add the 2 teaspoons of salt. Cover and set aside for at least 2 hours or, ideally, overnight.

2 Add the remaining ingredients to a saucepan and bring to a gentle simmer over a medium-low heat. Simmer for 10 minutes, then remove the pan from the heat and leave the pickling liquor to cool and infuse.

3 Drain the brined fennel and tightly pack it into a clean, sterilized jar or container with a tight-fitting lid. Pour over the cooled pickling liquid, herbs and spices included, ensuring the fennel is completely submerged.

4 Seal the jar or container tightly with the lid and place it in the fridge overnight to allow the flavours to intensify. The pickled fennel will keep in the fridge, unopened, for up to 3 months and up to 4 weeks in the fridge, once opened.

Spicy pickled carrots

MAKES 2 X 500ML/17FL OZ JARS

500ml/17fl oz white wine vinegar

100g/3½oz granulated sugar

1 teaspoon fine sea salt

1 teaspoon mustard seeds

2 garlic cloves, thinly sliced

1 teaspoon red chilli (hot pepper) flakes

500g/1lb 2oz carrots, peeled and sliced into sticks

1 Combine all the ingredients except the carrots in a medium saucepan with 250ml/9fl oz of water. Place the pan over a medium heat and bring the mixture to the boil, then reduce the heat and simmer for 5 minutes, stirring occasionally until the sugar and salt dissolve completely. Meanwhile, pack the sliced carrots into clean, sterilized jars or containers with tight-fitting lids.

2 Pour the hot pickling liquid into the jars, spices included, ensuring the carrots are completely submerged.

3 Seal the jars or containers tightly with the lids and let the contents cool to room temperature. You can eat the pickles straight away, but they will keep in the fridge, unopened, for up to 3 months and up to 4 weeks in the fridge once opened.

Pickled cauliflower

500ml/17fl oz white wine vinegar

100g/3½oz granulated sugar

1 teaspoon fine sea salt

1 teaspoon mustard seeds

1 teaspoon black peppercorns

3 garlic cloves, thinly sliced

500g/1lb 2oz cauliflower, broken into florets

MAKES 2 X 500ML/17FL OZ JARS

1 Combine all the ingredients except the cauliflower in a medium saucepan with 250ml/9fl oz of water. Place the pan over a medium heat and bring the mixture to the boil, then reduce the heat and simmer for 5 minutes, stirring occasionally until the sugar and salt dissolve completely. Meanwhile, pack the cauliflower forets into clean, sterilized jars or containers with tight-fitting lids.

2 Pour the hot pickling liquid into the jars, spices included, ensuring the florets are completely submerged.

3 Seal the jars or containers tightly with the lids and leave the contents to cool. Refrigerate the cauliflower for at least 24 hours, but ideally for a few days, to allow the flavours to develop before tucking in. The pickled cauliflower will keep in the fridge, unopened, for up to 3 months and up to 4 weeks in the fridge once opened.

Pickled red onions

500ml/17fl oz white wine vinegar

100g/3½oz granulated sugar

1 teaspoon fine sea salt

1 teaspoon black peppercorns

3 red onions, thinly sliced

MAKES 2 X 375ML/13FL OZ JARS

1 Combine all the ingredients except the onions in a medium saucepan with 250ml/9fl oz of water. Place the pan over a medium heat and bring the mixture to the boil, then reduce the heat and simmer for 5 minutes, stirring occasionally until the sugar and salt dissolve completely. Meanwhile, pack the sliced red onions into clean, sterilized jars or containers with tight-fitting lids.

2 Pour the hot pickling liquid into the jars, peppercorns included, ensuring the onions are completely submerged.

3 Seal the jars or containers tightly with the lids and leave the contents to cool. Refrigerate the red onions for at least 24 hours, but ideally for a few days, to allow the flavours to develop before tucking in. The pickled onions will keep in the fridge, unopened, for up to 3 months and will continue to develop flavour over time. Once opened, use within 4 weeks.

Pecorino Romano + rosemary crackers

Buffalo mozzarella + taralli

Gruyère + dark chocolate digestives

Gouda + multigrain crackers

Roquefort + rye crackers

Creamy soft cheese + charcoal crackers

Goat's cheese + classic flatbread crackers

Goat's cheese + fruit toast

Cheese and crackers are as loving a pairing as salt and pepper and sugar and spice, but crackers come in so many different shapes, sizes and flavour profiles these days that choosing which to pair with which cheese is an artform in itself – especially when their different colours, shapes and sizes can make such a visual impact on the board, too.

Crackers

BUFFALO MOZZARELLA & TARALLI
with roasted cherry tomatoes
• *Buffalo's milk* • *Mozzarella di Bufala DOP* • *1*

Enhance Taralli are like breadsticks but in little looped shapes that create a perfect mouthful. Made using wheat flour and olive oil, they have a tangy and rich flavour that perfectly enhances the rich creaminess of buffalo mozzarella.
Contrast Texture contrast is what works here. Buffalo mozzarella is a stretchy, soft cheese that collapses seductively when torn – the airy crispiness of these little breadstick bites ensures you appreciate that luxury in spades. It's one of my favourite appetizers.
Balance Mozzarella di bufala is sealed in a brine, which gives it a slightly salty edge. With sourness already in the cheese and the dry bitterness in the cracker, there is good balance overall in this pairing. Both elements are also mild in their flavours, ensuring neither overpowers the other.

GOAT'S CHEESE & CLASSIC FLATBREAD CRACKERS
with grilled portobello mushrooms & sage
• *Goat's milk* • *Ragstone* • *2*

Enhance Lightly salted olive-oil flatbreads are the key here, bringing out the salty tang in the goat's cheese, making it especially moreish.
Contrast Goat's cheese's creamy texture is well placed to contrast with the snap of flatbread crackers. My favourite here is Ragstone, which has a slightly denser, more lingering texture than other, similar cheeses. This works particularly well with these crackers, giving plenty of bite and chew to each mouthful.
Balance Choose a flavourful goat's cheese for this pairing, with exceptional lemony tang, as in my favourite. A greater intensity in the cheese holds its own for good balance with the texture and sweet olive-oil flavour of the flatbreads.

ROQUEFORT & RYE CRACKERS
with caramelized onions
• *Ewe's milk* • *Roquefort AOP* • *4*

Enhance The pepperiness of the Roquefort finds a robust sponsor in the woodland flavour of rye crackers. Each of these brings out the boldness in the other.
Contrast Beautifully marbled with deep blue-green veins, Roquefort AOP has plenty of sharp, sour notes, which are offset against the earthiness in the rye.
Balance Rich and pungent, Roquefort has a deep, layered intensity that could easily overpower another cracker. Not so with hearty rye, which is a good match for the power in the cheese, while also providing just enough submission to let all the depth in the cheese shine through.

CREAMY SOFT CHEESE & CHARCOAL CRACKERS with truffle honey
• *Cow's milk* • *Saint-Marcellin* • *2*

Enhance The backdrop of the matte-grey charcoal crackers makes for a good-looking pairing with a creamy soft, pale cow's milk cheese such as Saint-Marcellin. The mild, slightly peppery spice flavour of the paste is lifted beautifully by the mild ash notes in the crackers.
Contrast Where the cheese gives a gently floral and sweet aroma, the crackers bring earthy, smoky depth. The contrast makes this a tempting pairing, long before it hits the palate.
Balance There's melt-in-the-mouth texture in this cheese, which has a slightly porous paste, to balance the dense snap of the crackers. They are well matched in intensity – this is a flavourful cracker and a flavourful soft cheese.

GRUYÈRE & DARK CHOCOLATE DIGESTIVES with apple

• *Cow's milk* • *Urs Leuenberger Le Gruyère Réserve* • *3*

Enhance Swiss Gruyère is known for its nutty tones, so paired with chocolate digestive it's like savoury meets confectionary, each enhancing the other to perfection.
Contrast Gruère is a particularly smooth cheese, texture-wise, with an almost waxy sheen. The crumbly crunch of a digestive makes for a delightful texture contrast that shows off this distinctive nature of the cheese beautifully.
Balance Chocolate brings bittersweet notes to this pairing, with the cheese giving deep savoury tones, a gentle bitterness and tang as you chew and a caramelly, rich, vanilla-sweet finish.

GOAT'S CHEESE & FRUIT TOAST with roasted peach

• *Goat's milk* • *Sinodun Hill* • *2*

Enhance This is a particularly good pairing if you can find a light, mousse-like goat's cheese with a hint of almond, as in Sinodun Hill. That nuttiness is brought out gorgeously by the fruit toast.
Contrast Hold the cheese in your mouth for a moment to release its delicate citrus layer, which contrasts so well with the intense sweetness of the fruit in the toast. This is a smooth and light cheese, so there is plenty of texture contrast, too.
Balance What a well-rounded pair! The cheese brings sour, sweet and salty, while the toast brings sweetness from the fruit and bitterness in the toasting. There's plenty of flavour intensity in the toast itself to stand up against a more flavourful soft goat's cheese.

GOUDA & MULTIGRAIN CRACKERS with cranberry chutney

• *Ewe's milk* • *Cornish Mature* • *4*

Enhance Multigrain crackers, rich with oils from the seeds, are a delicious way to enhance the buttery character of Gouda, as well as develop its nutty undertones.
Contrast Gouda is a smooth, hard cheese with a light crystalline crunch from the salt crystals that form during ageing. This gives it a delightful distinction against the crisp, nutty texture of the crackers.
Balance There's good balance of salt in this pairing, which gives an overall yummy, full-bodied savouriness. I love the hint of sweetness from the cheese's finish, too.

PECORINO ROMANO & ROSEMARY OLIVE OIL CRACKERS with truffle oil

• *Ewe's milk* • *Pecorino Romano* • *5*

Enhance The salty finish of these crackers (see page 74) is a perfect way to enhance the layers of robust savouriness in Pecorino Romano.
Contrast Hard and crumbly, Pecorino Romano needs the firm, secure crunch of these crackers to give a good texture contrast and enjoyable mouthfeel. I also love the way the herbiness of the rosemary contrasts so confidently with the spicy sharpness in the cheese.
Balance These are all the flavours of Italy, so the pairing brings balance of terroir and climate, as well as taste. Bittersweet olive oil, aromatic rosemary, salty, spicy and sour Pecorino that bursts with umami – it's an Italian fusion that scores on every level.

Rosemary olive oil crackers

Crackers are incredibly simple to make, making them a must for a bespoke cheese pairing. These crackers have a subtle sweetness, fresh rosemary, plenty of oil and the perfect salty finish. They are altogether an ideal partner for Pecorino Romano (see page 72).

MAKES 25–30

125g/4½oz plain (all-purpose) flour

125g/4½oz wholemeal rye flour

1 teaspoon light brown soft sugar

3 tablespoons finely chopped rosemary leaves

2 tablespoons olive oil

1 teaspoon flaked sea (kosher) salt, plus optional extra to sprinkle

1 Preheat your oven to 250°C/230°C fan/500°F/Gas 9.

2 In a medium–large bowl, combine both flours with the sugar and rosemary. Pour in the olive oil and 125ml/4fl oz of water and stir the mixture together. You may need a splash more water if it is overly dry. When you can't stir any more, bring the dough together with your hands, and knead gently until smooth.

3 Place the dough in the centre of a large sheet of floured parchment paper and cover with a second sheet of parchment. Using a rolling pin, roll out the dough between the two sheets of parchment to about 3mm/⅛in thick. Peel off the top piece of parchment and use it to line a large baking sheet. Trim the edges of the cracker dough with a large knife, then cut the dough into evenly sized squares, each about 5cm x 5cm (2in x 2in).

4 Using a palette knife, transfer the squares to the prepared baking sheet and sprinkle the tops with a little more sale, if you like. Bake for 15–20 minutes, or until golden. Remove the crackers from the oven and transfer them to a wire rack to cool and harden. They will keep in an airtight container for up to 5 days.

Homemade chocolate digestives

It might not be unusual to see plain digestives on a cheeseboard, but I love these dark, homemade digestives as an alternative. Cheese and chocolate is itself such a good pairing that they bring all-round harmony to the palate, with the biscuit bridging the gap between rich, dark chocolate and your favourite cheeses – Gruyère in the case of our board.

MAKES 10

180g/6¼oz wholemeal flour

40g/1½oz plain (all-purpose) flour

75g/2½oz caster (superfine) sugar

½ teaspoon baking powder

a pinch of fine sea salt

150g/5½oz unsalted butter, cubed and chilled

75g/2½oz 70% dark (bittersweet) chocolate, finely chopped

cold water, if necessary

FOR THE CHOCOLATE COATING

150g/5½oz 70% dark (bittersweet) chocolate, finely chopped

30g/1oz unsalted butter, cubed and chilled

1 Combine the dry ingredients in a large mixing bowl, then add the butter. Rub it into the dry flour mixture with your fingers until the mixture resembles coarse breadcrumbs. This should take 5–10 minutes. Stir in the chopped dark chocolate until evenly distributed.

2 Bring the mixture together until it forms a dough, you may need to add a splash of cold water to help bind the dough if it is a little dry.

3 Dust a large sheet of parchment paper with flour and place the dough in the centre. Cover with a second large sheet of parchment paper and roll it out between the two sheets. When the dough is about 3mm/⅛in thick, carefully peel off the top sheet and use it to line a large baking sheet.

4 Using a 7cm/2¾in cookie cutter or an equivalent-sized glass rim, cut out rounds from the dough. Use a palette knife to carefully transfer the biscuit rounds onto the prepared baking sheet, ensuring that they are spaced well apart. You can re-roll the trimmings to cut more rounds, if you wish. You should be able to make about 10 biscuits altogether.

5 Prick each biscuit with a fork or skewer to create the classic digestive biscuit pattern, then put the baking sheet in the fridge for half an hour to allow the digestives to firm up.

6 Meanwhile, preheat your oven to 180°C/160°C fan/350°F/Gas 4. Once the raw digestives have chilled, bake for approximately 15–20 minutes, or until they turn golden brown. Remove them from the oven and transfer to a wire rack to cool completely. (They will harden as they cool.)

7 To make the chocolate coating, melt the chocolate and butter together in a heatproof bowl set over a saucepan of gently simmering water. Stir the mixture as it melts. Once fully melted and combined, remove the bowl from the pan and leave the coating to cool slightly for 5 minutes.

8 Dip the biscuits into the chocolate to half coat them. You can either dip them face down for a classic finish or edgeways for a modern take. Place on a wire rack, set over a tray to catch any drips, then transfer to the fridge for 30 minutes, or until the chocolate has hardened. Store the biscuits in an airtight container for up to 7 days.

Manchego + sea salt
70% dark chocolate

Soft cheese +
milk chocolate

Roquefort
+ chilli
70% dark
chocolate

Cheddar + milk
chocolate
coated nuts

Camembert +
hazelnut dark
chocolate

Parmesan + dark
chocolate orange

Cheese and chocolate might not immediately spring to mind as a perfect pairing, but certain flavour notes make them great bedfellows – creamy, salty, bitter, rich... all these are words that we frequently use to describe each independently. In this board, we bring them together to amazing effect.

Chocolate

SOFT CHEESE & MILK CHOCOLATE
with caramel drizzle
• *Cow's milk* • *Waterloo* • *2*

Enhance Both elements in this pairing have a distinctive milky flavour and texture – enjoying them together creates a luxurious tasting experience, with pillows of creaminess.
Contrast The cheese itself has contrast between its bright white rind and rich, yellow paste – which contrasts again with the darkness of the chocolate.
Balance There's lovely balance here. The cheese has just enough edge to its creaminess to provide a foil for the sweetness in the smooth chocolate.

MANCHEGO & SEA SALT 70% DARK CHOCOLATE with Marcona almonds
• *Ewe's milk* • *6 months mature* • *3*

Enhance Both Manchego and dark chocolate have an intensity that sit well together. The cheese brings out the bittersweet strength in the chocolate, while the sea salt enhances the tangy saltiness of the cheese.
Contrast A defining characteristic of Manchego is its slightly sweet edge, which nicely complements the sugar notes in the dark chocolate. Both also offer contrasting savouriness – from the nutty, earthy flavours in the cheese and the rich, forest-floor quality in the chocolate.
Balance Choosing sea salt dark chocolate makes this an exceptionally well-rounded pairing to give a pleasing flavour experience on the tongue, while the creamy base to the cheese helps to balance out the tartness.

GOAT'S CHEESE & WHITE CHOCOLATE
with fresh figs
• *Goat's milk* • *Valençay* • *3*

Enhance Valençay has plenty of delicate, creamy notes and the sweet, silky allure of white chocolate is perfect for bringing these to the fore. Together, they create a luxurious and delightful taste experience.

Contrast White chocolate is known for its intense sweetness, which provides an exceptional contrast to this tangy cheese.
Balance Valençay has a slight acidity, owing to the style in which it's aged, which balances perfectly with the white chocolate's sweetness.

ROQUEFORT & CHILLI 70% DARK CHOCOLATE with honey
• *Ewe's milk* • *Roquefort AOP* • *4*

Enhance There is a delicious, strong tang in Roquefort, and chilli dark chocolate is the perfect way to highlight that characteristic. Together they elevate and intensify the spiciness in each other.
Contrast Here, contrast comes from the texture. Each mouthful of Roquefort gives way to creaminess on the tongue, while bitter chocolate provides a quiet snap.
Balance This pairing is the master of harmony! Roquefort's tanginess and creaminess balance perfectly with the chocolate's sweetness and the chilli's heat.

CHEDDAR & MILK CHOCOLATE-COATED NUTS with dried cranberries
• *Cow's milk* • *Pitchfork Cheddar* • *3*

Enhance Cheddar gives rich, nutty notes, which the chocolate-coated nuts bring to the fore. The sweetness of the chocolate is there to offset and enhance.
Contrast Sweet and earthy chocolate meets tangy and earthy Cheddar. The way the topnote flavours contrast makes for an exciting taste experience.
Balance The Cheddar and chocolate-coated nuts strike a perfect balance: salty and sweet; tangy and earthy; deeply savoury and gently bitter.

Try also:
Camembert & hazelnut dark chocolate with toasted baguette
Cashel blue & chocolate brownie with fresh cherries
Parmesan & dark chocolate orange with candied peel

Chocolate salami

This sweet beauty, studded with nuts and orange zest and offering a hit of ginger, pairs exquisitely with semi-hard, mild blue cheeses such as Fourme d'Ambert or Rouge Creamery Smokey Blue. It is also beautiful with aged gouda, as the rich, caramelized notes and nutty undertones of the cheese complement the indulgent sweetness of the chocolate, whilst adding a savoury element. I particularly love this after dinner as a dessert–cheeseboard combo.

MAKES 1 LOG

175g/6oz ginger biscuits, bashed into small chunks

100g/3½oz chopped nuts (such as pistachios, almonds or hazelnuts)

85g/3oz crystallized ginger, chopped

zest of 2 oranges

200g/7oz 70% dark (bittersweet) chocolate, chopped

100g/3½oz salted butter

2 tablespoons golden (light corn) syrup

a pinch of fine sea salt

1 In a large mixing bowl, combine the crushed ginger biscuits, nuts, crystallized ginger and orange zest and set aside.

2 In a medium heatproof bowl set over a saucepan of gently simmering water, melt the chocolate, butter and golden syrup together. Gently stir until fully melted and combined, then add the sea salt and remove the bowl from the heat.

3 Pour the melted chocolate mixture over the biscuit mixture and stir through until well combined – it will be very thick.

4 Place a large sheet of parchment paper on a clean work surface and transfer the chocolate mixture into the centre. Using the parchment to help you, shape the mixture into a uniform log roughly 30cm/12in long, wrapped in the paper. You'll need to gently roll the 'salami' back and forth in the parchment to help shape it. Twist the ends to seal and chill the salami in the fridge for 2 hours, or until set.

5 To serve, place it on a board and slice it into thin rounds.

Colombian hot chocolate with gooey cheese

In Colombia, hot chocolate is a beloved beverage enjoyed throughout the year. This traditional drink combines the rich flavours of dark (bittersweet) chocolate with the surprising addition of mozzarella – the result is a truly creamy delight.

SERVES 2

480ml/16½fl oz whole milk

70g/2½oz 70% dark (bittersweet) chocolate, chopped

1½ tablespoons granulated sugar

30g/1oz hard (cooking) mozzarella, cut into 2cm/¾in cubes

1 Pour the milk into a medium saucepan and place the pan over a low heat. Gently warm the milk, stirring continuously, until it is hot, but not boiling – until small bubbles form around the edge of the pan and steam starts to rise from the milk.

2 Add the chocolate to the pan and stir continuously until the chocolate has fully melted and blended with the milk. Stir in the sugar, until dissolved, then keep stirring until the mixture comes to a simmer.

3 Place half the mozzarella cubes into each serving mug, then carefully pour half the hot chocolate mixture into each, leaving the delicious, silky hot chocolate to melt the cheese for 2–3 minutes before serving and enjoying straight away.

Goat's cheese
+ honeycomb

Blue cheese +
truffle honey

Gouda +
honeybee pollen

Camembert
+ hot honey

No two honeys are the same – the flora from which the bees collect their pollen gives every honey a uniqueness directly related to its provenance. Here, though, I'm looking to honeys scented with fruit, fungi and flowers, as well as the delicious notion of homemade sugary honeycomb. It's not really true honey, but it is sooooo good with cheese!

Honey

GOAT'S CHEESE & HONEYCOMB
• *Goat's milk* • *Sainte-Maure de Touraine* • 2

Enhance The fizz on the tongue of sweet honeycomb picks out those lemony flavours of a soft, young goat's cheese to perfection.
Contrast Crunch and creamy here for contrast. Crumbly honeycomb highlights the intense creaminess of a goat's cheese. Sainte-Maure de Touraine is a semi-firm log that melts in the mouth – the yielding of the honeycomb crackle and sumptuous cheese together is truly something else.
Balance Ash-rinded Sainte-Maure de Touraine has earthy, woody notes that bring a level of nuttiness to this party. There's a good balance from the cheese's sharp bite and the honeycomb's intense sweetness.

BLUE CHEESE & TRUFFLE HONEY
• *Cow's milk* • *Perl Las* • 1

Enhance I utterly love truffle honey – it combines all the sweet and earthy flavours that are also so redolent in cheese. In this pairing, it's that earthiness that brings out the earthiness in a mild, young blue – Perl Las (meaning 'Blue Pearl') is a perfect example.
Contrast This is where the intense sweetness of truffle honey comes through – to contrast with that savouriness imparted by the dotted blue veins in the cheese. The stickiness of the honey is a lovely foil, without jarring, against the creamy texture of the paste.
Balance Perl Las has a mellow, salty and creamy paste with a long, heady aftertaste that's balanced by the sweet and sharp flavours of the honey. Umami abounds.

GOUDA & HONEYBEE POLEN
• *Cow's milk* • *Dutch Farmhouse* • 5

Enhance Honeybee pollen is little orbs of earthy sweetness, which are wonderful for bringing out the sugary notes in a farmhouse Gouda.

Contrast The precise nature of the floral hints in honeybee pollen will depend upon where the bees have been foraging for their gold, but whatever the exact flavour profile, the heady meadow tones will always contrast with the sharp, aged flavour profile of an extra-mature cheese to create a sense of both light and dark in one bite.
Balance Crunchy, intense and tangy, aged Gouda is well-balanced in both flavour and texture against the sweet earthiness of the bee pollen. There's bitterness in this pairing, too, so roundedness is built-in.

CAMEMBERT & HOT HONEY
• *Cow's milk* • *Isigny Sainte-Mère* • 5

Enhance Is there anything more decadent and luscious than extra-mature Camembert? And particularly Isigny Sainte-Mère? Silky, equally luscious hot honey is a partner made in voluptuous heaven.
Contrast The spice of the hot honey in this pairing squares up so well to the intensely savoury, tangy cheese. That spice cuts through the creaminess to make sure that the pairing feels opulent and not cloying.
Balance Oh so much savoury umami here! Isigny Sainte-Mère is a particularly protein-rich Camembert that gives it mushroomy umami in spades. The land, near the sea, where the cattle graze gives the cheese a particularly mineral, earthy quality that is well matched for its natural tanginess. Sweetness, of course, comes from that wonderful honey.

Try also:
Beaufort & salted honey
Chèvre & lavender honey
Gorgonzola dolce & acacia honey
Ricotta & raw orange blossom honey
Taleggio & chestnut honey

Easy homemade honeycomb

Honeycomb (so easy to make at home!) transforms and elevates the flavour and texture in creamy goat's cheese – it is sweet crunch to the cheese's tangy earthiness. Try it with a gorgeous creamy cheese like sinodun hill or Golden Cross. It makes for a delightful contrast of sweet and savoury on your palate.

MAKES 1 LARGE SLAB

100g/3½oz caster (superfine) sugar

4 tablespoons golden (light corn) syrup

a pinch of fine sea salt

1½ teaspoons bicarbonate of soda (baking soda)

1 Line a 20cm x 30cm (8in x 12in) baking sheet with parchment paper. Set aside.

2 Combine the sugar, syrup and salt in a small saucepan and place the pan over medium-low heat.

3 Stir the mixture gently until the sugar dissolves. Then, stop stirring and let the sugar boil until it turns a deep amber colour. This should take only about 3–4 minutes, so keep an eye on it as you don't want it to burn. Once the sugar mixture has turned amber, immediately remove the saucepan from the heat and quickly add the bicarbonate of soda, stirring it in gently but swiftly. The mixture will start to foam, then expand (take care as it can splutter and spit).

4 Carefully pour the mixture onto the baking sheet – you can spread it out slightly using a spatula, just don't push it down too much, as you want the bubbles. Leave the honeycomb to cool and set for 30–60 minutes at room temperature (the time will depend on how warm your kitchen is). Once it's hardened, break it into smaller pieces using your hands or a knife. The honeycomb will keep in an airtight box for up to 14 days.

Fiery hot honey

Brie and Camembert are the exciting pairs for this dynamic condiment, delivering an electrifying fusion of sweet and heat to your palate. It's the hard-hitter on a cheeseboard that makes everyone go 'wow!'

MAKES 1 X 240ML/8FL OZ JAR

240ml/8fl oz runny honey

2 teaspoons dried chilli (hot pepper) flakes

1 red chilli, deseeded and finely chopped (optional)

1 tablespoon apple cider vinegar

1 In a saucepan, combine the honey and chilli flakes, and red chilli, if using. Place the saucepan over medium heat and bring the mixture to a simmer, then immediately remove the pan from the heat.

2 Stir in the apple cider vinegar to combine. Strain the hot honey into a sterilized glass jar, seal with a lid and store for up two months. Refrigerate once opened.

Cheddar +
piccalilli

Chèvre +
lavender honey

Gouda + seville
orange marmalade

Pecorino + damson
fruit paste

Blue cheese +
orange ginger
chutney

Appenzeller
+ spiced
honey mustard

Halloumi +
apricot jam

Camembert +
raspberry jam

There are some pungent flavours on this cheeseboard, because once you introduce the sweetness of jam, the spice of chutney and the tang of pickle to a pairing, the robust flavours of some of our smelliest cheeses can really sing. Don't forget – start with the mildest and work up to those big guns, for the full effect.

Jams & chutneys

GOUDA & SEVILLE ORANGE MARMALADE
• *Cow's milk* • *Boerenkaas* • *3*

Enhance The caramelized undertones of the cheese come to the front and centre when paired with the deeply bittersweet, burnt-orange flavour of Seville orange marmalade.
Contrast Texture provides good contrast in this pairing – the marmalade is sticky on the tongue, with chewy flecks of the bitter orange, while smooth Gouda provides a decadent silkiness.
Balance There is a wonderful balance of summer sunshine in this pairing. The Gouda comes from the milk of cows that have grazed on Dutch meadows rich with summer flora, while the Seville orange marmalade is infused with the heat of southern Spain. Each complements the other in perfect harmony.

CAMEMBERT & RASPBERRY JAM
• *Ewe's milk* • *Camembert de Normandie AOC* • *5*

Enhance Each of the components in this pairing bring the aromas of the countryside to your cheeseboard. Camembert, with its earthy, mushroomy and pungent notes is reminiscent of the farms on which its made; while raspberry jam reminds us of the sweet, tart freshness of the fields and forests.
Contrast The buttery, rich and pungent aromas in Camembert find the ultimate foil in the heady sweetness of raspberry jam.
Balance Camembert de Normandie has quite a distinctive chocolate-hazelnut quality in its flavour, which is lusciously balanced with the sweet tartness of raspberries. It's like the perfect savoury–sweet dessert.

HALLOUMI & APRICOT JAM
• *Ewe's and/or goat's milk* • *Odysea Premium Sheep or Goat's Milk Halloumi* • *1*

Enhance A good halloumi is delicate in flavour, with mildly nutty undertones and a zesty freshness that is characteristic of its young age. It's that tanginess that apricot jam – at once tart and sweet – is so good at bringing out of the cheese.
Contrast Salt and sugar contrast beautifully in this pairing – the natural saltiness of halloumi loves to both intensify the sweetness of the apricot jam and counter it. Equally that delicious squeakiness in the halloumi's texture is contrasted so well in the sticky jam.
Balance Halloumi and apricots have a common denominator in the climate and terroir of Cyprus, which makes these two a natural match made in heaven – savoury meets sweet, nutty meets fruity, giving overall balance in both flavour and aroma.

GRUYÈRE & TOMATO JAM
• *Cow's milk* • *Västerbottensost* • *4*

Enhance Each element of this pairing brings out the tanginess in the other. A slice of Västerbottensost, a speciality Gruyère made in Sweden (rather than the traditional Switzerland), topped with a spoonful of tomato jam sets the tastebuds alight.
Contrast Caramelized and toffee-like, the lingering flavours of this cheese come into playful opposition with the fresh spiciness of a tomato jam – choose one with a hint of ginger to add a pleasant heat to your palate.
Balance Gruyère is a 'plump' and chewy cheese, with typically more than 30-per-cent fat content, that needs the tartness of the tomato jam to give it a rounded and balanced mouthfeel.

SOFT CHEESE & CHILLI JAM
• *Goat's or cow's milk* • *Rocamadour AOP or Saint-Félicien* • *2*

Enhance Saint-Félicien, a cow's milk soft cheese from the French Alps, has a mildly tangy quality that is encouraged to shine against the delicate sweet-spice of a chilli jam. Similarly the Rocamadour, from the Lot region in southwest France, has that underlying zestiness you expect from a goat's cheese, which the chilli helps to shine.

Contrast There are lots of contrasts in flavour and texture in this pairing, but for me it's the bright red–orange, flecked with deeper red, of the jam against the creamy white of the cheese – that really gets my taste buds ready for a delicious mouthful. And they look so gorgeous against one another on a board.

Balance I love the balance of the velvety rich soft cheese with the loose, jelly-like nature of chilli jam in this pairing, while the buttery, creamy and delicate cheese is pepped up by the spice in the finish.

PECORINO & DAMSON FRUIT PASTE
• *Sheep's milk* • *Pecorino di Pienza* • 3

Enhance This is an enhancement of riches! Damson fruit paste is an intensely decadent condiment, with deep, plum-pudding notes. Pecorino di Pienza is deeply rustic and luscious, a semi-hard cheese that just adores soaking up those strong, fruity flavours.

Contrast This particular style of Pecorino is aromatic with wild herbs, which serves as a foil for the rich, cloying fruit of the paste – and, of course, vice versa.

Balance The cheese itself is particularly balanced in its flavour – with salty, sour and bitter notes all unleashing themselves on the palate as the cheese melts in the mouth. The sweetness, though, is more subtle, so introducing a pairing that draws out that herbal freshness (think sweet, young peas rather than sugar) helps everything to work together.

BLUE CHEESE & PEAR, ORANGE & GINGER CHUTNEY
• *Cow's milk* • *Montagnolo Affine* • 5

Enhance The spicy notes in a blue cheese such as Montagnolo Affine, a slowly ripened, blue-marbled cheese from Germany, are brought to life when paired with a chutney laced with the gently warming heat of ginger. Delicious!

Contrast Sweet and sour aromas are the order of the day here. I love the way the chutney itself offers sweet and bitter all in one, which contrasts so well with the buttery tangy of the cheese.

Balance For me, pears (along with figs) are the fruit that have a magical quality to make almost any cheese sing – but particularly blue cheese. In this pairing, adding the zestiness of the orange, the heat of the ginger and sweetness of the pear to the overall umami in the cheese is just ultimate harmony on a board.

CHEDDAR & PICCALILLI
• *Cow's milk* • *Westcombe Cheddar* • 5

Enhance The acidity in the piccalilli is a master at making sure you get the full force of the tang in a super-mature Cheddar as soon as the aromas hit your nose.

Contrast While there is sourness in abundance in this pairing, I love that the cheese itself also offers an underlying caramel sweet note that makes a welcome contrast.

Balance Earthy, with a robust and nutty flavour, extra-mature Cheddar, especially that from Westcombe, brings an abundance of savouriness to this pairing. That makes the sweet, sour and bitter tones in the piccalilli a perfect balance to all that aged complexity.

APPENZELLER & SPICED HONEY MUSTARD
• *Cow's milk* • *Appenzeller Extra (Appenzeller Exquisite)* • 4

Enhance The rind of this cheese is washed in a spiced brine that imparts its own spiciness to the cheese. Pairing with a spiced honey mustard makes the most of this unique quality.

Contrast This cheese is intensely tangy, but as honey mustard is more sweet than it is sour, the two make a perfect foil for one another.

Balance Tasting notes for Appenzeller include green apple, vibrant herbs and roasted nuts – fresh, fruity, earthy and smoky all in one. With the spice and sweetness of the condiment at the same time, the overall finish on the palate lingers in delicious harmony.

CHÈVRE & LAVENDER HONEY
• *Goat's milk* • *Sinodun Hill* • 5

Enhance This cheese is produced to remain as true as possible to the flavour of its milk, from goats fed in the South Oxfordshire countryside. The result is a light and lemony paste that is lifted with the tangy qualities of the honey.

Contrast Aerated to be almost cloud-like, the texture of this goat's cheese is beautifully set against the oozy, dense texture of the honey in this pairing.

Balance The intensely floral notes of lavender honey bring wonderful balance to the longlasting finish of this goat's cheese. The meadows of Oxfordshire are discernible in every bite.

Try also:
Blue cheese & pear jam
Goat's cheese & fig jam
Triple cream & plum chutney

Cherry compôte

The symphony of cherries, vanilla and lemon in this compôte harmonizes perfectly with Valençay, mascarpone and Chèvre cheeses. Overall, it's a combination that makes a tantalizing contrast to celebrate the artistry of cheese and condiment.

MAKES 1 X 300G/10½OZ JAR

500g/1lb 2oz cherries, pitted and halved

1 vanilla pod, seeds scraped, pod and seeds reserved

150g/5½oz granulated sugar

juice of 1 lemon

1 Place the halved cherries in a medium saucepan and add both the vanilla seeds and the empty pod. Add the sugar and lemon juice, then place the pan over a medium heat, stirring to combine the ingredients. Leave the mixture to come up to a gentle simmer, stirring occasionally to dissolve the sugar. Once the sugar has dissolved, reduce the heat to low and leave the cherries to simmer for 15–20 minutes, or until they are soft and have released their juices. You may need to stir the compôte occasionally to stop it catching on the bottom of the pan.

2 Once the cherries are soft and the syrup has thickened to a loose jam consistency, remove the pan from the heat and discard the vanilla pod. Pour the into a sterilized jar and seal with a lid. It will keep unopened for up to 12 months, or up to a 3 months open in the fridge.

Fig jam

My homemade fig jam is a mixture of plump figs, zesty lemon and a hint of vanilla. This delightful preserve is beautifully paired with the rich, fruity notes of blue cheese.

MAKES 1 X 375G/13OZ JAR

900g/2lb figs, destemmed and cut into 1cm/½in pieces

300g/10½oz caster (superfine) sugar

60ml/2fl oz lemon juice

½ teaspoon orange zest

¼ teaspoon vanilla extract

1 In a large saucepan, combine the fig pieces with the sugar, and place them over a medium-low heat for about 15 minutes, stirring occasionally, until the sugar has mostly dissolved and the figs release their juices.

2 Add the lemon juice, orange zest and vanilla extract and 120ml/4fl oz of water to the pan, increase the heat to high and bring the mixture to the boil, stirring continually until the sugar has fully dissolved.

3 Reduce the heat to medium and simmer, stirring occasionally, until the fruit becomes soft and the liquid thickens, running off the side of a spoon in thick, heavy drops (this should take about 20 minutes). Spoon the prepared fig jam into a sterilized jar with a tight-fitting lid. Seal the jar securely and leave the jam to cool to room temperature. The jam will keep unopened for about 12 months, or 3 months in the fridge once opened.

Cheese *and* drink pairing

Gorgonzola dolce + Moscato d'Asti

Manchego + red Rioja

Brie + Champagne

Blue Stilton + port

Chèvre + Grüner Veltliner

Roquefort + Sauternes

Pecorino Toscano + Sangiovese

Époisses + Pinot Noir

I love cheese and I love wine and when I put them together, I'm in heaven. These are the power couples of the cheese-pairing world, and I've had so much fun considering the terroir, aromas, textures and flavours of both to make sure each pairing works decadently together. There are some classic combos here (think Stilton and port), as well as some more surprising ones – for example, Chèvre is often paired with Sancerre, but I love the way Grüner Veltliner brings out its fresh acidity. Nibble, sip and enjoy!

Wine

ÉPOISSES & PINOT NOIR
with micro herbs
• *Cow's milk* • *Berthaut Époisses 'Perrière'* • *2*

Enhance Époisses, from Burgundy, pairs impeccably with the Pinot Noir red wine from that region. Pinot Noir's silky, lighter weight and ripe red fruit flavours soften the bold pungency of the cheese to release layers of complex flavour that have earthy undertones and hints of cured meat.
Contrast The spicy, salty flavours in the cheese contrast beautifully with Pinot Noir's delicate raspberry and cherry fruit characteristics.
Balance Pinot Noir is a lighter weight wine and this combines well with Époisses' creamy, powerful texture giving an experience that is fully rounded on the palate.

ROQUEFORT & SAUTERNES
with cherry jam
• *Ewe's milk* • *Roquefort Carles* • *3*

Enhance I love pairing blue-veined cheeses with sweet wines and there's no more sublime a match than Roquefort with Sauternes. The luscious sweetness and acidity of Sauternes really releases the creamier, sweeter finish that hallmarks Roquefort Carles, especially.
Contrast This is a classic sweet and salt contrast – the cheese's bold, blue edge foiling the wine's indulgently rich depth of flavour.
Balance Sweet (from the wine) and sour (from the cheese) find equilibrium in this pairing. The intensely strong and salty notes in the cheese are tamed by the sweetness of the wine for ultimate balance of power.

BRIE & CHAMPAGNE with fresh strawberries
• *Cow's milk* • *Brie de Meaux Dongé* • *2*

Enhance Champagne is a classic match with brie and, ideally, I would choose a Blancs de Blancs (made using only Chardonnay grapes) and Brie de Meaux Dongé for the perfect combination. The crisp freshness of the wine enhances the rich, powerful flavours of the brie, while the bubbles cleanse the palate of the fats and protein in the cheese.
Contrast Champagne is high in acidity and with each sip, the crispness of the wine cuts through the creamy richness of the cheese.
Balance Blancs de Blancs Champagne exhibits flavours of stone fruits, brioche and vanilla and these balance perfectly with the creamy, mushroomy notes in the brie. Neither overpowers the other; both sing.

PECORINO TOSCANO & SANGIOVESE
with honeycomb
• *Ewe's milk* • *Pecorino Toscano* • *4*

Enhance Pecorino Toscano, known for its firm texture and nutty flavour, pairs brilliantly with the earthy aromas of Sangiovese, most notably in the wines of Chianti. Together, the tannins of Sangiovese cling to the proteins of the cheese, enhancing the sour-cherry fruit character of the wine and richness of the cheese.
Contrast I love how Pecorino's firm, buttery texture contrasts with the wine's high acidity and medium body.
Balance The bittersweet finish on a Sangiovese wine is perfectly weighted against the lingering umami in the cheese, with its hints of sheep's milk on the palate.

BLUE STILTON & PORT
with dark-chocolate-dipped figs
• *Cow's milk* • *Cropwell Bishop Stilton* • 4

Enhance Renowned for its rich, tangy flavour, Cropwell Bishop Stilton relishes the honey sweetness of the Port to bring out its slightly spicy, long finish.
Contrast The high alcohol of Port kicks back against the buttery heart of this cheese to make sure there is nothing overpowering in such a rich combination.
Balance Spicy and sweet dominate this pairing in perfect balance. Meanwhile, both give a suede-like mouthfeel that is impossible to resist.

GORGONZOLA DOLCE & MOSCATO D'ASTI with fresh pear
• *Cow's milk* • *Gorgonzola al Cucchiaio* • 3

Enhance Moscato d'Asti, a sweet white wine from northern Italy with gentle bubbles and a delicate grape flavour, is all about enhancing the underlying sweetness of the cheese for a fresh, lively pairing.
Contrast The light fizz of the wine contrasts with the cheese's luscious creaminess and rich flavours. My favourite here is so creamy and soft, its name means 'of the spoon'!
Balance The low alcohol and pure, rounded fruit of the Moscato d'Asti work help to cut through the richness of this flavourful cheese to create perfect balance.

CHÈVRE & GRÜNER VELTLINER
with toasted almonds
• *Goat's milk* • *Banon* • 2

Enhance Austrian Grüner Veltliner is known for its white-pepper notes, which sprinkle themselves deliciously over the vegetal, woody flavours of the goat's cheese, bringing out its zing.
Contrast The zesty acidity and tart fruit of the Grüner Veltliner makes for a distinct and lively dance with the creamy texture of the cheese.
Balance Primarily this pairing is about balancing acidity: my favourite cheese here, Banon Chèvre, has a tanginess that needs the zesty crunch of acidity you get from the wine to achieve harmony. The result is invigorating and well-rounded.

MANCHEGO & RED RIOJA
with chorizo
• *Ewe's milk* • *La Oveja Negra* • 4

Enhance Manchego, celebrated for its nutty and slightly salty notes, is a classic partner to the Tempranillo grape, at the heart of Rioja wines. For my favourite, La Oveja Negra Manchego, the tannins in Rioja align with the protein in the cheese to reveal a sublimely sweet, savoury complexity.
Contrast Herbaceous and deeply savoury notes in the Manchego sit juxtaposed with the red fruits and leather notes of the wine to create a delicious interplay of grassy, fruity and rich.
Balance Manchego has a firm texture that marries beautifully with Rioja's velvety tannins while the red fruit flavours harmonize with the cheese's nutty richness, creating a smooth and refined combination.

GRUYÈRE & PINOT NOIR
with fresh apple
• *Cow's milk* • *Gruyère AOC* • 4

Enhance Pinot Noir grapes produce lighter, fruitier, elegant reds – ideal for bringing out the slightly sweet profile of a good Gruyère.
Contrast The cheese's firm and slightly crystalline texture contrasts beautifully with the wine's soft tannins and enticingly perfumed, summer fruit flavours.
Balance Both cheese and wine in this pairing have a fruity character that is well balanced in strength and aroma. A light Pinot Noir red will likely have a floral, raspberry character that is reminiscent of the floral character in the cheese. Both have a silkiness that works sumptuously together.

Confit potato & cream cheese canapés

Confit potato cubes topped with a luscious and tangy cream cheese and lemon mixture. The crowning touch comes from a luxurious dollop of caviar or fish roe, adding a burst of flavour and sophistication. Garnished with fresh chives, these canapés are the epitome of elegance.

MAKES 12

4–5 large potatoes, peeled and cut into 2.5cm/1in cubes

225g/8oz duck fat or 225ml/7½fl oz olive oil

4–5 garlic cloves, crushed

2–3 thyme sprigs, leaves picked

115g/4oz full-fat cream cheese, beaten until soft

1 tablespoon lemon juice

about 4 tablespoons caviar or fish roe

sea salt and freshly ground black pepper

a few chives, chopped, to garnish (optional)

1 Preheat your oven to 140°C/120°C fan/275°F/Gas 1.

2 Combine the potato cubes, duck fat or olive oil, garlic cloves and thyme leaves in an ovenproof dish. Season with salt and pepper, then cover the dish with foil or a lid and place it in the oven. Cook the seasoned potatoes for about 2–3 hours, or until the potatoes are tender when pierced with a fork.

3 While the potatoes are confiting, prepare the cream-cheese topping. In a small bowl, mix together the cream cheese and lemon juice, and season with salt and pepper to taste.

4 Remove the cooked potatoes from the oven and drain away the excess duck fat or olive oil. Leave the potatoes to cool slightly before you begin assembling the canapés.

5 To assemble, place a small spoonful of the cream cheese topping on each potato cube, then top with a small dollop of caviar or fish roe. Sprinkle with chives, to garnish, if using, then serve immediately.

Wine pairing: These canapés cry out for a glass of Champagne in the other hand! The acidity of Champagne can help cleanse the palate and provide a refreshing contrast to the creaminess of the delectably cheesy mouthfuls.

Époisses fondue with wine

Époisses cheese is well known for its strong flavour – and aroma ... the reason it's prohibited on some public transport in France. However, when it's baked, this cheese becomes rich and creamy, which makes it a perfect base for a wine fondue, scooped with steamed potatoes. Perhaps unexpectedly, the wine in this fondue is red – made from Pinot Noir grapes, which give fruity and earthy notes that balance the richness of the cheese.

SERVES 2

2 x 250g/9oz Époisses cheeses, in their wooden boxes

200ml/7fl oz Pinot Noir wine

1 onion, sliced into rings

350g/12oz baby new potatoes, steamed until tender

1 Preheat your oven to 200°C/180°C fan/400°F/Gas 6.

2 Remove any plastic or paper wrap from the cheeses and place the naked cheese wheels back in their round wooden cases. Carefully wrap the wooden cases in tin foil, taking care not to cover the cheeses themselves.

3 Use a knife to gently puncture the surface of each cheese. This allows them to breathe. Divide the onion rings into two equal portions then spread them over the top of each the cheeses. Pour the wine equally over the cheese and onions (the flavours will meld together during baking).

4 Place the cheese-filled wooden boxes on a baking sheet and put them into the preheated oven. Bake the cheeses for 20 minutes, until they bubble and go gooey inside.

5 Serve the baked Époisses alongside the steamed potatoes for dipping.

Buffalo mozzarella + pilsner

Gorgonzola piccante + Belgian dubbel

Double cream brie + Belgian triple

Old Amsterdam + amber ale

Saint-Nectaire + bitter

Camembert AOC + saison

Blue cheese + stout

Cheddar + IPA

Ales, lagers and ciders can be as rich and diverse in complexity as wine, which makes pairing them with cheese an equally exciting adventure. Here, I've taken ten different styles of beer and paired them with ten very different cheeses to demonstrate how the texture, effervescence and flavour profile of everything from cider to Belgian Trappist beers to a light pilsner can find its match in an enticing cheeseboard.

Beer

SAINT-NECTAIRE & BITTER with salted nuts
• *Cow's milk* • *Saint-Nectaire Fermier* • *2*

Enhance A strong bitter is the perfect complement for the rich and robust flavours of this semi-soft, washed-rind cheese. The hoppy, dark flavours of the beer are thankful for the cheese's deep savouriness.
Contrast Frothy, effervescent bitter is a great foil for the smooth, creamy texture of the cheese.
Balance Spicy and nutty with an edge of saltiness, Saint-Nectaire is well balanced against dark, hoppy flavours of the bitter. The earthiness of this beer is well matched to the mushroom notes in the cheese.

CHEDDAR & IPA with multigrain crackers
• *Cow's milk* • *Hafod* • *4*

Enhance The deeply earthy, even oniony aromas in a good, strong Cheddar are well matched in the grittily hoppy aroma of an IPA.
Contrast Sour and bitter tastes rub up against each other here – strong Cheddar cheese has a sharp, citrussy character and flavour, while the IPA is deeply bitter.
Balance I love how the rich, buttery texture of the cheese gives way to a meltingly moreish salty tang, which, with a sip of IPA, transforms to deep, mushroomy umami.

BLUE CHEESE & STOUT with honey
• *Cow's milk* • *Stichelton* • *4*

Enhance Stichelton is one of my dad's favourites. It is a bold blue cheese, whose rich and nutty flavour is elevated by a glass of chocolatey, buttery stout.
Contrast The deep-roasted notes in the stout contrast well with the crisp tang of the blue veins in the cheese.
Balance Most stouts have a dried-fruit flavour that imparts sweetness to counter the layers of bitter hops and roasted coffee. In order for the stout not to overpower, the cheese needs to be robust of its own accord and the meaty, strongly savoury flavour of Stichelton is just the ticket for holding its own.

GOUDA & AMBER ALE with 70% dark chocolate
• *Cow's milk* • *Old Amsterdam Gouda* • *5*

Enhance Old Amsterdam is a rich Dutch Gouda with caramel notes that cling to the malty richness of the beer, bringing them to the fore.
Contrast An aged Gouda's firm and crystalline texture (particularly in the case of Old Amsterdam) is offset by the beer's malty sweetness and gentle fizz.
Balance This is a strong-flavoured cheese with hints of Marmite and nuts – amber ale's malty, robust flavours are important as they stand up to and embrace the cheese's intensity.

CAMEMBERT AOC & SAISON with red grapes
• *Cow's milk* • *Camembert de Normandie AOC* • *4*

Enhance A refreshing saison pale ale, with its spicy, fruity style, is brilliant at developing the Camembert's rounded, buttery flavours.
Contrast In this pairing, contrast is all about texture: Camembert with its soft, velvety creaminess is perfectly foiled by the effervescent bubbles of the saison.
Balance I love how the cheese's mild earthiness and the beer's fruity freshness create a satisfying weight in your mouth. Their aromas are well-balanced, too – the mushroomy undertones of Camembert de Normandie bring out the sweet fragrance in the beer and the cheese's own salty, grassy and bitter notes.

Try also:
Buffalo mozzarella & pilsner with cherry tomatoes
Double-cream brie & Belgian tripel with honeycomb
Gorgonzola piccante & Belgian dubbel with candied pecans

Beery cheese dip

This delicious dip marries the rich flavours of Cheddar, Gruyère and Saint-Nectaire with the effervescence of lager beer. The result is a gooey, flavourful dip. I like soft, salty pretzels as my dipper.

SERVES 2–4

60g/2oz unsalted butter

2 tablespoons plain (all-purpose) flour

240ml/8fl oz lager

360ml/12½fl oz single (light) cream

1 teaspoon Dijon mustard

1 teaspoon Worcestershire sauce

¼ teaspoon garlic powder

½ teaspoon fine sea salt

¼ teaspoon cayenne pepper

100g/3½oz mature Cheddar, grated

100g/3½oz Gruyère, grated

80g/2¾oz Saint-Nectaire, grated

1 tablespoon chopped chives

pretzels, for dipping

1 Melt the butter in medium saucepan over a medium heat. Add the flour and whisk to incorporate, then continue whisking continuously for 1 minute – this 'cooks out' the floury flavour. Still whisking continuously, little by little add the lager and cream, to make a smooth sauce. Then, whisk in the Dijon mustard, Worcestershire sauce, garlic powder, salt and cayenne pepper until well combined.

2 Bring the mixture to the boil, whisking continuously so that no lumps form, then reduce the heat to a simmer. Continue cooking, now whisking frequently, until the sauce thickens – about 3 minutes.

3 With the heat on low, a handful at a time, add the cheeses, whisking between each addition and ensuring each handful of cheese is fully melted and incorporated before adding more. Transfer the beery cheese dip to a bowl, sprinkle with the chives and serve warm with pretzels for dipping.

Cider mac 'n' cheese

Think cheese and apple, but with melty cheese, apple cider and delicious pasta in a moreish, grown-up twist on a classic mac 'n' cheese. I can't think of anything more comforting. Bake it to crispy, golden perfection.

SERVES 4

350g/12oz dried elbow macaroni or spirali

35g/1¼oz unsalted butter, plus extra for greasing

50g/1¾oz plain (all-purpose) flour

400ml/14fl oz whole milk

100ml/3½fl oz dry (hard) apple cider

1–3 teaspoons English mustard paste (depending how hot you want it)

2 tablespoons double (heavy) cream

150g/5½oz mature Cheddar (I like Montgomery Cheddar), grated

3 tablespoons fresh breadcrumbs (optional)

fine sea salt

1 Preheat your oven to 200°C/180°C fan/400°F/Gas 6 and grease a roughly 20cm x 30cm (8in x 12in) baking dish with a little extra butter.

2 Bring a large saucepan of salted water to the boil. Add the macaroni and boil it for a little less time than it states on the packet instructions, until it is just slightly undercooked. Drain and set aside.

3 While the pasta is boiling, make the sauce. Melt the butter in medium saucepan over a medium heat. Once melted, add the flour and beat with a wooden spoon to incorporate to a smooth paste, known as a roux. Cook for a minute or two to 'cook out' the floury flavour, then remove the pan from the heat.

4 Little by little, add the milk to the roux, stirring well after each addition to a smooth, lump-free sauce. Once you have added all the milk, add the cider – again, little by little, incorporating it gradually while the pan is off the heat and stirring thoroughly between each addition.

5 Return the pan to a medium heat and bring the mixture to a gentle boil, stirring continuously throughout. Reduce the heat and add the mustard 1 teaspoon at a time – tasting the sauce as you go to make sure the mustard isn't overpowering, but has presence. Add the cream and stir to combine.

6 Set aside a small handful of the cheese for the topping, then add the remainder to the sauce in the pan, stirring to melt. Taste the sauce again and adjust the mustard, if necessary.

7 Tip the macaroni into the pan with the sauce and stir to combine, making sure all the pasta is coated. Transfer the mixture to the prepared dish and sprinkle over the breadcrumbs (if using) and the reserved cheese. Pop the dish in the oven and bake for 20–25 minutes, until the sauce is bubbling and the top is golden brown and crispy. Serve immediately.

Buffalo mozzarella
+ aperol spritz

Cheddar +
whiskey sour

Gorgonzola +
negroni

Brie + french 75

It's party time with this cheeseboard! There are so many good, delicious and moreish pairings here, I defy you not to find everyone cancelling the cabs and dancing the night away in your living room. Wine and cheese is great. Cocktails and cheese are another level.

Cocktails

BRIE & FRENCH 75
• *Cow's milk* • *Brie de Meaux* • *1*

Enhance To France, with the lemon juice in the French 75 (combining also gin and the decadence of Champagne) making sure to highlight the zesty notes at the edges of this mild brie.
Contrast Oozy, soft and unctuous brie gets its lively opposite in the bubbles of the Champagne.
Balance Gin gives the French 75 its strength – peppery, herbaceous and botanical, the spirit offers a robust backdrop to the mild, spring-onion-like qualities of a young brie.

GORGONZOLA & NEGRONI
• *Cow's milk* • *Gorgonzola naturale* • *1*

Enhance Negroni is an intensely bitter and alcoholic aperitivo, made with equal parts Campari, gin and sweet vermouth. The bitterness is just what this Gorgonzola needs to bring out its biting quality, cutting through the creaminess of the paste.
Contrast The fiery alcohol of the Negroni is restrained by the milky mouthfeel of this mild Gorgonzola.
Balance The Negroni's citrussy aroma, thanks to the traditional orange-peel garnish and the oils it imparts, provides roundedness. The sweet-sour notes balance the bitterness in the other elements of the cocktail and the earthy, savoury notes in the aroma of the cheese.

CHEDDAR & WHISKEY SOUR
• *Cow's milk* • *Lincolnshire Poacher* • *5*

Enhance A good strong Cheddar (I'm choosing Lincolnshire Poacher here, although strictly it isn't a Cheddar but it has all the qualities of a phenomenal one; see page 15) has exactly the acidity and tanginess that this cocktail needs to complement its sour flavours – in the whiskey and the lemon juice.
Contrast Hold a piece of strong Cheddar on your tongue and as it melts; you'll find an underlying nutty sweetness in its aroma that lingers in the finish. The

Whiskey Sour lives up to its name (not only in the lemon juice, but in the whiskey itself), so take a sip after that finish and enjoy the contrast.
Balance Not only does egg white bring the drink its characteristic froth, its creamy, meringue-like flavour tempers all that sourness. The soft froth itself balances out the harsh intensity of the alcohol.

APPENZELLER & GIN MARTINI
• *Goat's milk* • *Appenzeller Extra (Appenzeller Exquisite)* • *5*

Enhance Appenzeller is known for its mineral, herbaceous flavours, which come to the fore when paired with the medicinal botanicals of gin.
Contrast The touch of sweetness is Appenzeller (or other Swiss cheese – some more so than others) helps to temper the harsh bitterness of this classic cocktail.
Balance The surgical precision of the flavours in a Martini cut through the characteristic oily elasticity of Appenzeller to ensure there's no danger of feeling overwhelmed by the mouthfeel as you eat and sip.

BUFFALO MOZZARELLA & APEROL SPRITZ
• *Buffalo's milk* • *Mozzarella di Bufala DOP* • *1*

Enhance Breathe in from the top of the Aperol bottle and you'll be hit by the intense bitter sweetness of orange. Buffalo mozzarella has a very slight acidity that the Aperol Spritz helps to bring through.
Contrast The texture of the bubbles – in a glorious pop-popping of fizz on your tongue – is a great foil for the creamy softness of this decadent, enveloping cheese.
Balance Creamy mozzarella finds its balance in the pear fruits of a Prosecco and citrus fruits in the Aperol. This is a phenomenally well-rounded cheese-and-cocktail pairing, if ever there was one.

Try also:
Goat's cheese & Moscow Mule
Gouda & Old Fashioned

Parmesan espresso martini

Don't judge this one before you try it. This cocktail is a beautiful fusion of cheesy richness and invigorating coffee, promising an experience that defies expectations and most definitely leaves a lasting impression.

SERVES 1

50ml/1¾fl oz vodka

25ml/1fl oz espresso

25ml/1fl oz coffee liqueur

25ml/1fl oz simple syrup

15g/½oz Parmesan, grated, plus optional extra shavings to garnish

ice cubes

1 Pour the vodka, espresso, coffee liqueur and simple syrup into a cocktail shaker and add the grated Parmesan. Three-quarters fill the shaker with ice cubes, then pop on the lid and shake vigorously for about 15–20 seconds to chill the mixture and incorporate the flavours.

2 Strain the cocktail into a chilled martini glass and garnish with the Parmesan shavings for an extra flourish, if you wish. Serve and enjoy this unique combination in a glass!

Sparkling apple ginger fizz

Embrace the sparkle of this refreshing mocktail, with its zest coming in bucket-loads from the lemon juice and ginger (which also brings a pleasant spice), but tempered with sweetness from the apple juice and honey. Over ice, served long, it's the best thing for a summer cheese platter.

SERVES 1

150ml/5fl oz cloudy apple juice

20ml/¾fl oz freshly squeezed lemon juice

2 teaspoons runny honey

ice cubes

50ml/1¾fl oz ginger beer

apple slice and mint sprig, to garnish

1 Put the apple juice, lemon juice and honey in a cocktail shaker, pop the lid on and shake well to combine.

2 Fill a highball glass with ice cubes and strain the mixture into it over the ice. Top up with the ginger beer and garnish with the apple slice and mint sprig. Serve immediately.

Citrus mint spritzer

If you're not looking for the spice that comes with ginger (see recipe above), this refreshing, zesty mocktail is a delicious alternative. It's great with most cheeses, but particularly with goat's or Pecorino.

SERVES 1

ice cubes

100ml/3½fl oz freshly squeezed orange juice

50ml/1¾fl oz freshly squeezed lime juice

20ml/¾fl oz agave syrup

soda water, for topping up

orange and lime slices and mint sprig, to garnish

1 Three quarters fill a highball glass with ice cubes. Pour in the orange and lime juices and the agave syrup and stir to combine. Top up the glass with soda water, then decorate the glass with slices of orange and lime and a sprig of mint.

Gjetost + Norwegian coffee

Swiss cheese + mocha

Goat's cheese + green tea

Cheddar + english breakfast tea

Brie + capuccino

Blue cheese + espresso

In Scandinavian *kaffeost,* a cube of 'bread cheese' is dropped into a mug and hot, black coffee is poured over – the cheese becomes melty and soft, taking on the flavours of the coffee, while the coffee absorbs hints of the cheese's nutty saltiness. I'm extending this tradition here, with suggestions for other coffee or tea and cheese pairings.

Coffee + tea

GJETOST & NORWEGIAN COFFEE
• Goat's & cow's milk • Ski Queen, Gjetost cheese • 1

Enhance There's a treacly aroma to this cheese, which is rich and dark and picked out perfectly by the viscous, smooth tones of Norwegian coffee.
Contrast Bitter notes in Norwegian coffee are well placed to contrast with the sweet, caramelized notes of Gjetost, a 'brown cheese' also from Norway.
Balance Bringing balance to this pairing are the lighter, fruity notes in Norwegian coffee, which isn't as strong or intense as coffees made in other parts of the world.

BLUE CHEESE & ESPRESSO
• Cow's milk • Fourme d'Ambert AOP • 5

Enhance At least 28-days matured, Fourme d'Ambert is a subtle Alpine French blue cheese with a silken texture that is well pepped with a shot of hot, sweet espresso.
Contrast I utterly love the creaminess of this cheese, which is a good antidote to the bite of espresso.
Balance Buttery, rich and tangy, with a hint of sweetness, and bags of powerful umami, add the bitterness of an espresso and you have the perfect balance of tastes in this pairing.

BRIE & CAPPUCCINO
• Cow's milk • Coulommiers • 1

Enhance A Brie-de-Meaux-style cheese, and similarly rich with a high milk-fat content, Coulommiers has a youthful, buttery texture that is the perfect way to make the most of the creaminess of a cappuccino.
Contrast A first sip of cappuccino, with the bitter cocoa topping and the bitter coffee slipping through the clouds of frothy milk, is countered with Coulommiers's caramelized onion notes – this cheese, particularly, has an underlying sweetness to its earthy profile.
Balance The nutty aroma of mild brie-style cheeses helps to marry bitter notes with sweet and creamy across this pairing, so that the overall experience is richly well-rounded.

GOAT'S CHEESE & GREEN TEA
• Goat's milk • Ticklemore • 3

Enhance Green tea's lighter, floral character is just the thing to bring out Ticklemore's fresh and grassy notes.
Contrast With its slightly dusty, fluffy mouthfeel, Ticklemore's texture contrasts well with the hot, thin zestiness of the green tea.
Balance Tasting notes for green tea (herbaceous, nutty, fresh, floral) match beautifully with the nutty, woodland and tangy characteristics of Ticklemore, and it's barely-there goatiness.

SWISS CHEESE & MOCHA
• Cow's milk • Gruyère • 3

Enhance The milky-chocolate nuttiness of mocha is a great way to bring out the nuttiness in a Swiss Gruyère.
Contrast A medium Gruyère still holds the freshness of Alpine-Swiss spring meadows on which the cows graze to sit against the autumnal warmth of a mocha.
Balance An aged Gruyère has a developing tangy, sharp flavour that sits comfortably against the creaminess of a mocha to make sure that neither the cheese becomes too harsh on the palate, nor the drink too cloying.

CHEDDAR & ENGLISH BREAKFAST TEA
• Cow's milk • Montgomery Cheddar • 5

Enhance Bold meets bold in this pairing. English breakfast tea's underlying lemony notes are a great way to pick out the zinginess in a well-aged Cheddar.
Contrast Mature Cheddar has a crumbly texture that contrasts well with the smooth tea. The salty notes in the Cheddar are a foil for the sweetness of the tea.
Balance Here, the tea offers both bitter and sweet, while the cheese brings sour, salty and heaps of umami. The result is a rich, perfectly rounded pairing.

Try also:
Cheddar & black coffee
Gouda & dark roast coffee
Tomme Crayeuse & matcha

Coffee cake with cream-cheese icing

Everyone assumes that cream-cheese icing is for carrot cake, but it's velvety, luscious and moreish on top of this moist, coffee-infused cake, too. Every bite is perfect harmony.

SERVES 6

180g/6¼oz salted butter, at room temperature, plus extra for greasing

165g/5¾oz light brown soft sugar

2 large eggs, whisked

180g/6¼oz self-raising flour

a pinch of fine sea salt

2 tablespoons freshly ground coffee, brewed in 100ml/3½fl oz just-boiled water

250g/9oz chopped walnuts or pecans

FOR THE CREAM-CHEESE ICING

500g/1lb 2oz full-fat cream cheese

1–2 tablespoons icing (confectioners') sugar, to taste

1 Grease 2 x 18cm (7in) sandwich tins with butter and line them, base and sides, with parchment paper.

2 Preheat the oven to 180°C/160°C fan/350°F/Gas 4.

3 In a large bowl, cream the butter and sugar together using an electric whisk until pale and fluffy. With the electric beaters still running, gradually pour in the whisked egg, a little at a time, until fully incorporated. Sift the flour and salt into the wet mixture and fold them through with a large spoon or spatula.

4 Line a sieve with a sheet of kitchen paper and strain the coffee into a small bowl. Add this into the cake batter, along with 200g/7oz of the chopped nuts, and fold through. Reserve the remaining nuts for decoration.

5 Divide the cake batter equally between the lined tins and bake the sponges for 30–35 minutes, or until a skewer inserted into the centre of each comes out clean. Once the sponges are out the oven, invert onto a wire rack to cool.

6 Meanwhile, make the icing. Add the cream cheese to a medium bowl and sift in 1 tablespoon of the icing sugar. Whisk well to combine. Taste the icing – if you like it sweeter, sift in the remaining icing sugar and whisk again to combine.

7 To assemble the cake, use a bread knife to remove roughly 3–4cm (1¼–1½in) of the domed top of each sponge (these are the chef's perks, so enjoy). Place one sponge the right way up on a cake plate, and spread one half of the cream-cheese icing over the top in an even layer, all the way to the edge. Top with the remaining sponge, upside down to give a perfectly flat top, then spread over the remaining icing. Decorate with the reserved nuts and serve.

World cheese pairing

Brie + honey

Valency + fig jam

Tomme de savoie + apricot jam

Tomme brûlée + cornichons

Sainte Maure de Touraine + Touraine wine

Roquefort + walnuts

Epposis + fig brûlée

The riches of France

When in France, one of my favorite things to do is sit outside a café, enjoying a beautiful cheese board and a large glass of wine. There's something special about the combination of the relaxed atmosphere, the delicious food, and the joie de vivre that makes this experience unmatched. Over the years, I have discovered some amazing cheese pairings that have become my go-to choices which I'm delighted to share with you here.

BRIE & HONEY
Cow's milk • Brie de Meaux AOC • 1

Enhance I've picked a mild French brie for this pairing, so that the honey – imbued with the meadow notes from the nectar that makes it – can bring out the young, floral and sweet notes in the paste of the cheese.
Contrast Like all bries, Brie de Meaux has a bitterness in the finish that is contrasted with the intense, lingering sweetness of honey. Those notes are evident in the aromas, before you even take a bite, too.
Balance I love how these two complement each other's stickiness – that oozing makes a great pair! Brie is deeply savoury, salty and sour, with that bitter finish, so once you bring in sweet from the honey, you have the perfect balance of flavour.

ROQUEFORT & WALNUTS
• Ewe's milk • Société Roquefort • 4

Enhance The cage-aged mould flavours of Roquefort receives complementary earthiness from nutty walnuts.
Contrast I love the contrast in colours here – Société Roquefort has a particularly pale paste that offsets the deep teal veining. Add the deep brown of walnuts (themselves creamy-pale inside) and this pairing is definitely a feast for the eyes, as well as the taste buds. There's texture contrast, too – with that soft, nutty crunch against the languishing softness of the cheese.
Balance A well-matched pairing lets neither overpower the other, and here Roquefort is a robust, complex and pungent cheese, but the savoury and bitter flavours of walnuts are a wonderful match.

TOMME DE SAVOIE & APRICOT JAM
Cow's milk • Tomme de Savoie PDO • 3

Enhance Subtle nuttiness is characteristic of the Tomme de Savoie, which comes from the French Alps, and is enhanced by the almond notes in the apricot jam.
Contrast Most tomme cheeses are made using semi-skimmed or skimmed milk, which makes them lower fat than other semi-soft varieties and lighter in overall experience. This gives good contrast against the richness of intensely sweet apricot jam.
Balance Aromas of deep earth and mushrooms from the cave-ageing of tomme de Savoie balance the floral, heady candy of apricot jam. Taste for the notes of citrus in the paste to give the element of sour.

CHÈVRE & ROASTED CONFIT GARLIC
• Goat's milk • Banon Fermier, Golden Cross or Vermont Creamery Coupule • 2

Enhance People often wince at the thought of eating whole cloves of garlic, but the cloves become sweet and rich through the process of confiting (in effect, preserving by simmering gently in oil), which brings out the sweetness in fresh goat's cheese.
Contrast Soft goat's cheese is famed for its citrus tang, which contrasts so well with the sweetness of the confit garlic. Banon Fermier is wrapped in chestnut leaves as it ages, giving a distinct freshness that contrasts with the earthiness of the garlic.
Balance The balance of textures in this pairing is exceptional – the cheese is soft and creamy, almost melting on your tongue while the garlic give a chewiness to give the effects a lingering finish.

Try also:
Cantal & cornichons
Epposis & fig brûlée
Mimolette & spicy mustard
Ossau-Iraty & brown butter fudge
Sainte Maure de Touraine & Touraine wine
Tomme brûlée & cornichons
Valency & fig jam

Brown fudge

This rich confection marries the depth of brown sugar with the creaminess of butter and evaporated milk. I like to cut mine into nine large squares, but 16 smaller ones is enough for a good bite each. The fudge pairs particularly well with Ossau-Iraty cheese (see pages 126–127).

MAKES 9–16 SQUARES

225g/8oz caster (superfine) sugar

225g/8oz light brown soft sugar

1 tablespoon glucose syrup

1 teaspoon flaked sea (kosher) salt

55g/2oz salted butter

400ml/14fl oz double (heavy) cream

vanilla extract

1 Line a 20cm/8in square cake tin or similar-sized dish with parchment paper.

2 Add everything but the vanilla extract to a medium saucepan and melt it all together over a medium-low heat. Once melted, stir the fudge mixture and turn the heat up to medium-high, bringing it all to the boil. Boil the mixture, stirring occasionally, until it reaches 114°C/237°F on a cooking thermometer, then remove the pan from the heat and let it sit for a couple of minutes to cool slightly.

3 Add the vanilla extract and, using a wooden spoon or spatula, stir the fudge mixture vigorously for about 20 minutes until it cools, loses its glossy shine and thickens to a very stiff paste. (This is a bit of a workout but the result will be worth it!)

4 Transfer the fudge to the prepared tin or dish, smoothing it out into the corners. Leave it for 2–3 hours at room temperature to harden and set. Then, turn out the fudge onto a board, peel off the parchment paper and cut it into squares. Store in a lidded container in the fridge for up to 4 weeks.

Fig brûlée

With their honeyed richness, caramelized figs beautifully complement the savoury, creamy and salty notes of myriad cheeses.

SERVES 4

8 figs, halved lengthways

8 teaspoons caster (superfine) sugar

1 Place the fig halves on a baking sheet, cut side upwards. Sprinkle each with ½ teaspoon of the caster sugar.

2 If you have a kitchen blow torch, carefully heat the sugar on top the figs, holding the torch flame close to the sugar until it melts and then caramelizes. Turn off the torch and leave the topping to harden until crisp, like the topping of a crème brûlée.

If you don't have a torch, heat the grill (broiler) to high. Once hot, slide the baking sheet under the hot grill and leave the figs for 5–6 minutes, or until the topping is crisp. Keep an eye on the figs, as you don't want the sugar to burn. As soon as it's melted, remove the figs from the grill and leave the topping to harden.

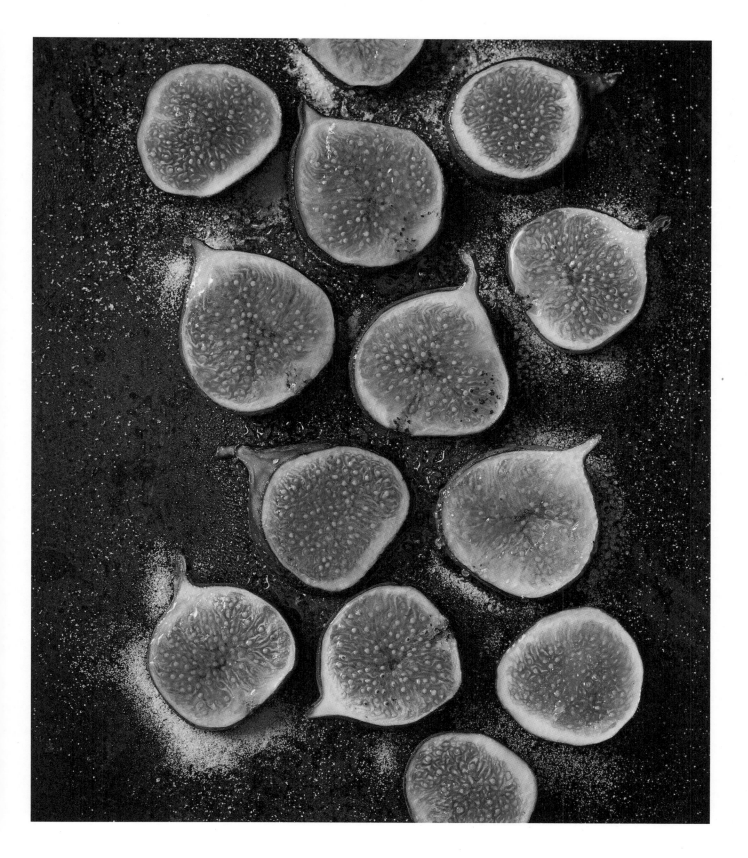

Cañarejal Cremoso + chorizo

Monte Enebro + rosemary crackers

Manchego + Serrano ham

Cabrales + fig and walnut cake

La Retorta + membrillo

Journey through Spain

There are some real treats on this board – taking you from the Basque country in northern Spain, through the valleys in the centre, to the warm, salty seashores of the Balearic island of Menorca. It's a pairing journey that calls on some pretty hefty flavours.

MANCHEGO & SERRANO HAM
• *Ewe's milk* • *Finca La Cuadra Reserva Manchego PDO* • 4

Enhance There's a gorgeous underlying sweetness to Serrano ham that makes it distinct from other cured meats. This brings out the caramel notes in the Manchego to utter perfection!
Contrast Manchego is such a deliciously bold cheese – tangy, intense and nutty with a firm, chewy mouthfeel. It makes a gorgeous contrast to the silky Serrano ham, which has a mellow and mild cured flavour.
Balance There's loads of savouriness going on in this pairing, which is why the undertones of sweet and salty in the ham and the sour and bitter notes in the cheese make for an exquisite roundedness in every mouthful.

TETILLA & SPANISH HONEY
• *Cow's milk* • *DOP Queixo Tetilla* • 1

Enhance Teaming Tetilla with Spanish honey allows the delicate floral, verdant forest notes of both to sing.
Contrast This young, soft cheese has a characteristically tart flavour that works in contrast to the sweetness of honey (and vice versa).
Balance Sour balanced by sweet, soft balanced with sticky, creamy balanced with viscous – there is roundedness at every turn here.

CABRALES & FIG AND WALNUT CAKE
• *Cow's/sheep's/goat's milk* • *Picos de Europa, Asturias* • 5

Enhance Wow! This is a strong one! The pungent aroma of a ripened Cabrales tells you it's blue long before you unwrap its regulation green-foil coat! Creamy, dry walnuts help to tempt out the cheese's own creaminess, beneath all those layers of powerful flavour.
Contrast Cabrales has high acidity, which is well contrasted by the bark-like bitterness of walnuts and the sweetness of the figs.
Balance I'm really keen on the balance of textures in this pairing – Cabrales melts beautifully which makes the chewiness of the fig and walnut cake a welcome bite.

LA RETORTA & MEMBRILLO
• *Ewe's milk* • *Cáceres, Extremadura* • 5

Enhance The quinces that make membrillo have a distinctive, heady floral quality – part rose, part pear – that is wonderful at bringing out the delicately herbal, grassy notes in this young cheese.
Contrast La Retorta is made using thistle rennet (making it suitable for vegetarians), which imparts a distinctive, pleasant bitterness in the finish. The intense sweetness of membrillo is a wonderful contrast.
Balance Rich, earthy and tangy, the paste of this cheese is so oozy that it almost flows as you cut into it. Balance that with sweet, sticky and chewy membrillo and I'm not sure there is anything more perfect.

MONTE ENEBRO & ROSEMARY CRACKERS
• *Goat's milk* • *Tiétar Valley, Ávila* • 4

Enhance This flavourful goat's cheese is encased in a mould-rich rind, which imparts intensely herbal, almost piquant notes. Pair this with the rosemary crackers and you are transported to the beautiful meadows of the Avila Valley, where this cheese is made.
Contrast The clean, lemony bite of this cheese contrasts with the underlying creaminess of the cracker, while also contrasting smooth (almost oozy), pearl-like paste with salty, crisp crunch.
Balance The lingering mushroomy notes of this exceptional cheese, made using only the best-quality milk from the herds grazing in the valley, bring plenty of umami savouriness to balance the salty, tart flavours in the cheese and bitter-herb notes of the crackers.

Try also:
Cañarejal Cremoso & chorizo
Idiazabál & chorizo
Mahón & Verdejo wine
Torta de Barros & roast ham

Spanish fig cake

Known in Spain as *pan de higo*, this traditional Spanish fig cake blends the sweetness of dried figs and dates with the nutty richness of almonds, all subtly kissed with honey, vanilla and cinnamon.

SERVES 2

400g/14oz dried figs (I like black Mission figs)

200g/7oz pitted dates

100g/3½oz raw, unsalted almonds, plus optional extra to decorate

1 teaspoon vanilla extract

2 teaspoons runny honey

a pinch of ground cinnamon

1 In a food processor, combine the dried figs, dates, almonds and vanilla extract. Pulse the ingredients until they are finely chopped and start to come together with a thick and sticky consistency. You may need to stop the food processor occasionally to scrape down the inside of the bowl. To help bind the ingredients further and add a touch of sweetness, drizzle the honey over the mixture in the food processor, then replace the lid and pulse a few more times.

2 Place a large sheet of parchment paper on a clean work surface. Transfer the mixture onto the paper in two equal portions and use your hands to mould and shape it into two, equal-sized 'cakes'. Sprinkle the cinnamon over the top of each cake to add a warm, aromatic flavour. I like to decorate the cakes with a few whole almonds at this point.

3 Transfer the cakes, on the parchment paper, to the fridge and chill them for 1 hour to firm up so that they hold their shape. Then, take the cakes out of the fridge and, using a sharp knife, cut them into small wedges – choose the size according to your own preference and intentions for cheese-pairing!

Orange membrillo

No Spanish cheeseboard would be complete without this traditional quince paste – but this version brings the twist of orange to the party for a particularly zesty edge that cuts through a little of the sweetness.

SERVES 2

2 large quinces, peeled, cored and chopped into 2cm/¾in chunks

zest and juice of 1 orange

500g/1lb 2oz granulated sugar

1 x 7.5cm/3in cinnamon stick

1 Put the quince chunks, orange juice and 500ml/17fl oz of water in a large saucepan. Place the pan over a medium heat and bring the liquid to a gentle simmer. Leave simmering for about 30–40 minutes, or until the quince chunks are tender and pierce easily with the prongs of a fork.

2 Carefully drain the quince pieces and transfer them to a food processor. Blitz them to a smooth purée, then return the puree to the pan. Add the sugar, cinnamon stick and orange zest to the quince purée and stir well. Place the pan on a low heat and cook, stirring frequently, until it takes on a deep orange hue and is thick enough that it holds its shape if you draw a wooden spoon through it. This will take about 1–1½ hours. You'll need to stir more frequently as the mixture thickens to prevent it catching and burning on the bottom of the pan. Remove the cinnamon stick from the mixture and bring the pan off the heat.

3 Preheat your oven to its lowest setting (usually about 70°C/50°C fan/150°F/Gas ¼) and line a shallow baking dish with baking paper.

4 Carefully pour the thick quince mixture into the lined baking dish, spreading it out in an even layer. Place the dish in the oven and leave the membrillo to dry out for several hours (this can take anything from 2 hours or so to overnight, depending on the natural pectin in the fruit), until the paste is firm to the touch. Once the quince paste has dried and set, remove it from the oven and let it cool completely before slicing into rectangles to serve. The membrillo will keep for up to 3 months in an airtight container in the fridge or 1 year in the freezer.

Pecorino Toscano + broad beans

Parmesan + aged balsamic vinegar

Fontina + mushrooms

Burrata + proscuitto

Mozzarella + tomato

Pecorino Siciliano + fig ball

Gorgonzola dolce + fresh peaches

This board brings together classic Italian pairings that are delicious just as they are, as part of a salad, or even melted into fondue-type decadence (Fontina cheese is perfect for this). Enjoy them all and every way.

Jewels of Italy

PARMESAN & AGED BALSAMIC VINEGAR
• Cow's milk • Parmigiano-Reggiano • 5

Enhance Balsamic vinegar (ideally from Moderna, and thick and viscous) and Parmesan are a classic combination because the balsamic chimes so beautifully with the sharp profile of the cheese.
Contrast Sweet with notes of cherry and butterscotch, aged balsamic helps to ground the complex tanginess of an aged Parmesan. They will set your taste buds alight.
Balance Umami-rich and nutty, Parmigiano-Reggiano welcomes the fruity notes in an aged balsamic, while the acid tames the saltiness in the finish of the cheese.

MOZZARELLA & TOMATO
• Buffalo's milk • Mozzarella di Bufala Campana DOP • 1

Enhance No Italian-centric cheeseboard is complete without this pairing! The acidic lift of perfectly ripe tomatoes helps to tempt out the gentle, lactic acidity of the buffalo mozzarella.
Contrast Again, the tomatoes' acidity, coupled with their sweet juiciness, cut through the creamy intensity of the cheese. On the tongue, that soft, tender, collapsing texture in the cheese is brilliantly offset by the crisp skin and burst of juice in the tomatoes.
Balance Tomatoes have natural umami, as well as sour and sweet. The buffalo mozzarella brings saltiness and a soft, bitter note, which sets it apart from cow's mozzarella. Together, the balance is perfect.

BURRATA & PROSCUITTO
• Cow's milk • fresh organic burrata • 1

Enhance There is a danger with burrata that the cream of the centre becomes sickly or cloying, but pairing with salty, cured prosciutto ensures that all the layers of flavour in this cheese are given a chance to shine. The prosciutto acts as salt does in any dish, tempting out the underlying flavours in the other ingredients.
Contrast Burrata has a spoonable consistency, but pair it with chewy, silky prosciutto and there is then plenty of texture to ensure you break down all those flavours as you eat to appreciate them fully.
Balance There is a subtle sweetness in burrata, and even a lemony twist – both of which find balance in the savouriness and salt of the cured meat.

FONTINA & MUSHROOMS
• Cow's milk • Val d'Aosta Fontina • 4

Enhance Chewy and robust, the textures in this pairing are a match made in heaven – both are dense and very slightly porous. The meatiness of the mushrooms is a perfect mirror for the smooth, semi-firm cheese.
Contrast Fontina begins its maturation with a distinctive, alpine freshness that underpins the flavours as the cheese matures to become earthier and fruitier. This freshness becomes more obvious when set against the undergrowth richness of the mushrooms.
Balance For me, the balance in this pairing is very distinctly in its marrying of the aromas of above and below ground. It feels like every breath and every mouthful captures the entire landscape, seen and unseen, of northern Italy's beautiful Aosta Valley.

PECORINO TOSCANO & BROAD (FAVA) BEANS
• Ewe's milk • Pecorino Toscano DOP • 2

Enhance This is a rustic pairing, bringing together two heroes of Tuscan home-style cuisine. Each offers both earthy and fruity, while the cheese adds a confident, dried-grass aroma and the beans contribute nuttiness.
Contrast Crunch meets smooth and bouncy in this pairing, as this young Pecorino has a semi-firm texture with pockets of air that keep it silky and malleable.
Balance The delicately creamy flavour of the beans and their fresh, springtime aroma help to balance the rich, sweet and tangy flavours of the cheese.

Try also:
Gorgonzola dolce & fresh peaches
Pecorino Siciliano & fig ball
Ricotta Mustia & grape juice

Cacio e pepe

Discover the magic of cacio e pepe, the classic Italian dish that celebrates the simplicity of cheese and pepper. For an added touch of visual appeal, I use a cheese wheel to create a unique serving experience. However, if a cheese wheel is unavailable, don't worry – the incredible flavours of this dish will still shine through however you serve it.

SERVES 2

1 small Pecorino Romano wheel or 90g/3¼oz Pecorino Romano, finely grated

250g/9oz fettuccine pasta

1 tablespoon freshly ground pepper

fine sea salt

1 If using, cut open the Pecorino cheese wheel by removing the top. Trace out a circle roughly 2.5cm/1in in from the outside of the cheese, then use a butter knife to begin removing chunks of the cheese by inserting the knife and pushing side to side. Keep the cheese chunks that you've removed in a separate bowl. You should only cut to a depth of about three quarters of the cheese wheel's overall height. Once you have a rough circular outline and have removed the top layer, switch to a spoon and begin to hollow out the cheese wheel to create a bowl.

2 Boil a large pot of salted water to cook the pasta. Once the water is at a rapid boil, place the pasta in the water and cook for a couple of minutes shorter than the packet instructions, until al dente.

3 If you're not using a Pecorino wheel, heat a large serving bowl.

4 Using tongs, transfer the cooked pasta directly from the pot into the cheese wheel. Mix the pasta inside the cheese wheel using tongs or by hand, ensuring the cheese melts and coats the pasta evenly. If the sauce looks dry, add a splash of pasta cooking water. The heat of the pasta will melt the cheese and create a creamy sauce. Alternatively, transfer the pasta to the warm serving bowl and add the grated Pecorino and a splash of pasta cooking water. Stir until the sauce emulsifies and creates a creamy sauce.

5 Add the black pepper to taste and continue mixing until well combined.

6 Serve the pasta directly from the wheel, allowing your guests to enjoy the experience of serving themselves.

Wine pairing - Vernaccia di San Gimignano. This Italian white wine from Tuscany complements the creamy and peppery flavours of the dish with its refreshing citrus notes. The Vernaccia di San Gimignano's bright acidity cuts through the richness of the cheese and enhances the peppery elements of the pasta.

My beautiful bruschette

Indulge in the irresistible allure of bruschette, a tantalizing spin on the timeless Italian appetizer, where velvety mozzarella, succulent tomato confit, vibrant pesto and crunchy pine nuts intertwine to create a seductive symphony of flavours, igniting your taste buds with every bite.

SERVES 4

4 slices of sourdough bread

250g/9oz buffalo mozzarella, or any other type of mozzarella, torn

20 confit tomato halves (see below)

4 tablespoons green pesto (see below)

2 tablespoons pine nuts

extra-virgin olive oil, for drizzling

a handful of rocket (arugula), to garnish

FOR THE CONFIT TOMATOES

400g/14oz cherry tomatoes

150ml/5fl oz extra-virgin olive oil

8 thyme sprigs

sea salt and freshly ground black pepper

FOR THE GREEN PESTO

30g/1oz basil

25g/1oz pine nuts

25g/1oz Parmesan, grated

1 garlic clove, peeled

juice of ½ lemon

extra-virgin olive oil

1 First, make the confit tomatoes. Preheat the oven to 140°C/120°C fan/275°F/Gas 1. Cut the tomatoes into halves or quarters, depending on their size, then place them on a baking sheet and drizzle them with the olive oil. Season with salt and pepper and sprinkle over the thyme sprigs.

2 Roast the tomatoes for about 2–3 hours, until they become soft and concentrated in flavour. Remove them from the oven and leave them to cool completely before using.

3 While the tomatoes are cooling, make the green pesto. Place the basil leaves and stems, pine nuts, Parmesan, garlic and lemon juice in a food processor. Pulse the ingredients while slowly drizzling in the olive oil through the feed tube until you have a smooth, loose paste (use a splash of water to loosen it, if necessary). Season with salt and pepper to taste.

4 To assemble the bruschette, first preheat the grill (broiler) to high.

5 Place the bread slices under the grill and toast them for 2 minutes on each side, or until golden and crisp. Arrange the mozzarella slices on the toasted bread and return the slices under the grill for 2 minutes, until the mozzarella is melted.

6 Remove the cheesy toasts from the grill and top each with a spoonful of confit tomatoes and a drizzle of pesto. Sprinkle with pine nuts and a splash of olive oil to finish. Garnish with rocket leaves and serve.

Wine pairing: Such a classic Italian dish deserves a classic Italian wine – I recommend Chianti Classico. This Italian red offers a medium body with moderate acidity, making it a versatile companion for a variety of dishes. In this case, its notes of ripe red fruits, herbs and earthy undertones will harmonize with the flavours of the bruschette.

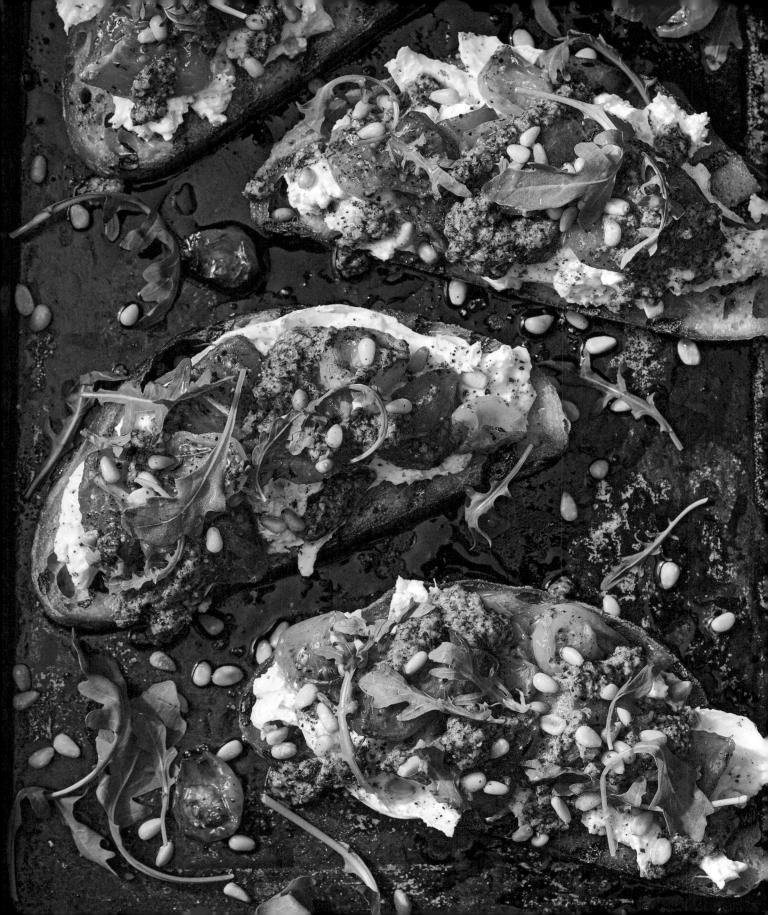

Prosciutto & peach sandwich with Gorgonzola butter

The salty and savoury flavour of the ham perfectly complements the sweetness of the peaches and the richness of the Gorgonzola butter in this sandwich with a distinctly Italian twist.

SERVES 1

125g/4½oz Gorgonzola dolce, at room temperature

100g/3½oz unsalted butter, softened at room temperature

1 tablespoon double (heavy) cream

1 teaspoon lemon juice

freshly ground black pepper (optional)

2 slices of focaccia bread

½ ripe peach, stoned and thinly sliced

2–3 prosciutto slices

1 First, make the butter. Put the Gorgonzola and butter in a mixing bowl and, using a hand mixer or a stand mixer fitted with the paddle attachment, whip the cheese and butter together until smooth and creamy. Add the cream and whip again until it is fully incorporated. The cream helps to lighten the texture and enhance the silkiness of the butter. Add the lemon juice and whip to incorporate fully (the lemon juice adds a tanginess that balances the richness of the dairy). Season with pepper, if you wish – it complements the flavour of the cheese and adds a bit of heat. Whip again until the butter is combined and light and fluffy.

2 Spread a generous layer of the Gorgonzola butter on each slice of focaccia, then place the remaining Gorgonzola butter in a container with a lid and store in the fridge for up to one week.

3 Top one buttered slice of focaccia first with the peach slices, then with the prosciutto. Carefully place the second slice of focaccia, buttered-side down, on top of the prosciutto to form a sandwich. Perfection.

Cabot clothbound Cheddar + caramel and herb popcorn

Rogue River Blue + fig paste

Rush Creek Reserve + warm crusty bread

Humboldt Fog goat's cheese + poached pears

This cheeseboard showcases some of the finest US cheeses available all over the world. Each has its own unique character, texture and flavour profile (there is an oozy, Vacherin-style, as well as a goat's, a Cheddar-style and a blue), beautifully paired with everything from pickles to popcorn!

USA road trip

HUMBOLDT FOG GOAT'S CHEESE & POACHED PEARS with honey
Goat's milk • Humboldt County, California • 3

Enhance Using poached pears for this duo is the way to make sure the special zestiness in this cheese shines through – everything is bringing sweet notes.
Contrast Humboldt Fog has a distinctive line of edible ash that runs through its paste, which in itself elevates the pasture-like goatiness and herbal qualities of the cheese's aroma. Introducing the festive, sweet spices of the poached pears ensures there is earthy sweetness that at once resonates and contrasts.
Balance Sour notes in both the cheese and wine, as well as bitterness from the ash, saltiness from the cheese, and sweetness from the pears and spices make this a truly well-rounded pairing.

RUSH CREEK RESERVE & WARM CRUSTY BREAD with truffle oil
Cow's milk • Uplands, Wisconsin • 2

Enhance Spoonability is what we're enhancing here. Rush Creek Reserve (like a Vacherin, from France) is an oozy soft cheese that, scooped on to pillows of warm, fresh bread, releases its lush, creamy texture and buttery richness in spades. Serving both elements warm from the oven elevates the decadence.
Contrast Crusty bread is essential for this pairing, so that there is a contrast in texture in every bite – crisp and crumbly gives way to soft, runny, deliciousness.
Balance Rush Creek has a complex savouriness that needs the gentle sweetness of the bread to bring balance in the overall experience. Anything too sweet would jar – bread has just enough sugar to find perfection.

ROGUE RIVER BLUE & FIG PASTE with crushed walnuts
• Cow's milk • Rogue Valley, Oregon • 4

Enhance This is a wonderfully complex cheese that is matured for up to 12 months and wrapped in pear-liqueur-laced vine leaves. I've opted to pair it with fig jam that asks us to look for the layers of sugary flavour imparted by the leaves and liqueur.
Contrast Like all blues, Rogue River Blue is fundamentally a salty, tangy cheese – flavours that in this case are bold and robust. The contrast of the intensely sweet fig jam makes us sit up and take note.
Balance Red-grape vine leaves (Syrah grapes, specifically) impart a full-bodied pepperiness to this cheese, which helps to balance out its sour, briny character. There is umami from the earthy, dark blue-green veins. I love the balance in textures – creamy paste with a little granular feel from the veins is well matched with the same qualities in the fig paste.

CABOT CLOTHBOUND CHEDDAR & CARAMEL AND HERBY POPCORN with hot honey
• Cow's milk • Jasper Hill, Vermont • 5

Enhance There's a fruity, sweet finish to Cabot Clothbound, aged for 10–15 months to develop a rich and complex savoury character. Popcorn laced with both caramel and herbs brings out all those qualities in this rich, flavourful cheese.
Contrast This Cheddar is known for its distinctively crumbly texture – beautifully contrasted with the firm crunch of the popcorn.
Balance This is a deep and rich Cheddar with a flavour intensity that's as powerful as it gets. Light, airy, sweet and herbal popcorn lifts all that earthy boldness to create a well-rounded pairing experience.

Try also:
Bonne Bouche & Sancerre with fruit toast
Harbison & duck pâté with baguette
Rush Creek Reserve & roasted root vegetables with crusty bread
Up in Smoke & salami with oatcakes
Winnimere & roasted grapes with crostini

Caramel & herby popcorn

Popping corn at home never stops being fun! In this recipe, I've avoided the need to choose between sweet or savoury and given this bowlful a hint of both – vanilla and syrup for the sweet, combined with herbs and salt for a savoury edge. It makes this a great accompaniment for Alpine-style US cheeses, and the contrast of textures is to die for. Make this for your ultimate movie night.

MAKES 1 LARGE BOWL

2 tablespoons flavourless oil, such as vegetable or rapeseed (canola) oil

75g/2½oz popcorn kernels

¼ teaspoon bicarbonate of soda (baking soda)

1 teaspoon vanilla extract

60g/2oz unsalted butter

100g/3½oz light brown soft sugar

2 tablespoons golden (light corn) syrup

1 tablespoon finely chopped herbs (I like rosemary, thyme or sage)

½ teaspoon fine sea salt, or to taste

1 Preheat your oven to 140°C/120°C fan/275°F/Gas 1. Line a baking sheet with parchment paper and set it aside.

2 Put the oil into a large saucepan with a tight-fitting lid and place it over a medium-high heat (leave the lid off for now). Once the oil is hot, add a few popcorn kernels and put the lid on the pan. Once the kernels start to pop, the oil is hot enough.

3 Remove the popped kernels from the pan and add the remainder. Cover the pan with the lid again and shake it gently to evenly distribute the heat. As the temperature increases inside the pan, shake it occasionally to prevent the kernels burning.

4 Once the kernels start popping, reduce the heat to medium and continue shaking the pan until the popping slows down. Remove the pan from the heat and let it sit for a minute to ensure all the kernels have popped.

5 In a small bowl, combine the bicarbonate of soda and vanilla extract, then set the bowl aside.

6 In a medium saucepan, melt the butter over medium heat. Add the

sugar and syrup, stirring until the mixture is smooth and combined. Bring the mixture to a gentle boil, then reduce the heat to low and let it simmer for about 2–3 minutes, stirring occasionally.

7 Remove the pan from the heat and stir in the bicarbonate of soda and vanilla extract mixture. Be cautious as the mixture will bubble and foam. Add the chopped herbs, stirring until they are evenly incorporated.

8 Pour the caramel herb mixture over the popped popcorn, gently stirring with a spatula to coat the popcorn evenly. Sprinkle the salt over the popcorn and give it another gentle stir. Transfer the coated popcorn to the prepared baking sheet, spreading it out in an even layer.

9 Place the baking sheet in the oven and bake the popcorn for 45 minutes, stirring every 15 minutes to ensure even baking, until it is golden and crisp. Remove the popcorn from the oven and let it cool completely on the baking sheet. It will keep in an airtight container for up to 1 week. Enjoy with your favourite cheeses.

White wine & brandy poached pears

Spiced poached pears is a classic dish that is traditionally served as a dessert however, the sweet and aromatic flavours also make it ideal for a cheeseboard. Here the white wine and brandy serve to bolster the flavour of the pears and add an additional level of flavour that works particularly well with goat's cheese.

SERVES 4

juice of 1 lemon

1 vanilla pod, split lengthways

250ml/9fl oz sweet white wine (such as Riesling or Moscato)

120ml/4fl oz brandy

55g/2oz light brown soft sugar

1 star anise

4 small pears (such as Bosc or Bartlett), peeled and halved

1 In a large saucepan, combine the lemon juice, split vanilla pod, sweet white wine, brandy, sugar and star anise. Place the pear halves into the saucepan, ensuring they are fully submerged in the liquid.

2 Place the saucepan over medium heat, bring the liquid to a gentle simmer, then reduce the heat to low and let the pears simmer gently for about 20–25 minutes, or until they become tender. Turn the pears occasionally to ensure even poaching.

3 Once the pears are tender, carefully remove them from the poaching liquid and set them aside on a plate.

4 Increase the heat under the pan to medium-high and bring the poaching liquid to a rolling boil. Let it boil until the liquid reduces and thickens slightly to a syrupy consistency (about 10–15 minutes). Remove the pan from the heat and strain the syrup through a sieve into a jug to remove the star anise and any other solids. Place the poached pears in a serving dish and pour the syrup over them.

5 Let the pears cool to room temperature, or refrigerate them for a few hours to chill, before serving.

Appleby's Cheshire + rhubarb compôte

Gorwydd Caerphilly + Welsh cakes

Eve goat's cheese + fresh grapes

Stichelton + caramelized walnuts

Stinking Bishop + caramelized onion chutney

Ogleshield + smoky bacon

Montgomery Cheddar + piccalilli

The first British cheeses are thought to have been crafted more than 2,000 years ago and it's now thought there are more than 700 cheeses produced here. I've gone with big, bold and robust flavours to demonstrate what an amazing array of delicious hard-hitters – from creamy brie-style to tangy blue – Great Britain has to offer.

Best of Britain

BARON BIGOD & BLACKCURRANT JELLY
• Cow's milk • Bungay, Suffolk • 5

Enhance Baron Bigod cheese, a brie-style cheese crafted in Suffolk, has a characteristically lingering finish. The sweet flavours of the jelly help to eke that out without letting it become heavy on the palate.
Contrast Rich and earthy meets sweet and floral in this pairing, giving the contrast of below and above ground in every bite.
Balance The rind of Baron Bigod imparts bold flavours of truffle and hazelnut, while the creamy, oozy centre is known for its lemony, zesty qualities. With the sweetness from the jelly, and just an edge of tang, the flavours are in perfect harmony.

TUNWORTH & SMOKED SALMON
• Cow's milk • Basingstoke, Hampshire • 5

Enhance Hand-crafted in Hampshire, Tunworth is Britain's answer to Camembert. Its wet-grass, mushroomy aroma is a perfect match for the burnt-wood flavours in the smoked salmon.
Contrast The paste of the Tunworth round has a fruity, slightly tangy quality that offsets beautifully against the richness of silky smoked salmon.
Balance Like so many Camembert-style cheeses, Tunworth carries with it a bold and pungent savouriness that holds its own against stronger accompaniments, such as smoked salmon. Its underlying sweetness, though, and gentle tang help to keep the whole pairing in balance.

STINKING BISHOP & CARAMELIZED ONION CHUTNEY
• Cow's milk • Dymock, Gloucestershire 5

Enhance Stinking by name and stinking by nature, here we have not just a bishop, but a king among British artisan cheeses. Its rind, washed in perry made using pears of the same name, imparts that distinctive aroma, but beneath that is a mild and sweet soft cheese that is beautifully enhanced with sweet onion chutney.
Contrast The paste of a Stinking Bishop is especially milky and creamy, and I love how the reassuring tang of the onion chutney contrasts with all that richness to make sure we go back for (plenty) more.
Balance This is a funky, earthy and complex cheese, so I'm keeping the pairing relatively straightforward to ensure a balance that doesn't complicate matters further. Onion chutney has a familiarness that is still bold enough to stand up to the cheese's might, but also knows its place.

APPLEBY'S CHESHIRE & RHUBARB COMPÔTE
• Cow's milk • Shrewsbury, Shropshire • 5

Enhance Appleby's Cheshire has such a beautiful orange–pink colour – a result of adding annatto, a natural colouring made using the seeds of the achiote plant, to the production process). To me this pairing is all about enhancing those hues to make an enticing, mouthwatering addition to the board.
Contrast This Cheshire has a distinctively crumbly texture that is well placed against the collapsing, decadent slump of a rhubarb compôte. That crumble gives way to the rhubarb on the tongue so that every mouthful feels like the warmest hug.
Balance There's so much complexity in Appleby's Cheshire – it is zesty and full-bodied in equal measure – that it finds its own balancing act beautifully. With the sweet-sharp accompaniment of rhubarb to mirror that harmony, this is a deliciously moreish pairing.

GORWYDD CAERPHILLY & WELSH CAKES

• *Cow's milk* • *Weston-Super-Mare, Somerset* • *5*

Enhance There is a characteristic lemony-ness to the paste of this cheese, which is lifted in the subtle, spicy notes of Welshcakes. If you can find freshly baked Welshcakes (or make your own!), snaffle them up – they are glorious.

Contrast This is a fresh, grassy cheese with a strong, complex flavour that shines against the sweet simplicity of a Welshcake.

Balance The long maturing period for Gorwydd Caerphilly (up to three months compared with a more usual one to two) results in a deep complexity of both flavour and aroma that brings sour, bitter and heaps of umami to every bite. Welshcakes have a richness that holds its own, while also bringing the intense sweetness of dried fruit and sugar.

OGLESHIELD & SMOKY BACON

• *Cow's milk* • *North Cadbury, Somerset* • *4*

Enhance There is a subtle meatiness to Ogleshield, a West Country cheese often likened to a Swiss Raclette, that laps up the chance to be paired with salty, sweet and smoky bacon.

Contrast The milky, creamy, melting texture of Ogleshield really shines against crisp bacon. A deliciously opposing pairing on a cheeseboard, but perhaps even better in a toastie!

Balance The saltiness of bacon brings balance for the creaminess of this cheese, while both bring sour notes and heaps of umami. All bacon, but especially smoked, has a sweetness that's so delicious on the palate.

MONTGOMERY CHEDDAR & PICCALILLI

• *Cow's milk* • *North Cadbury, Somerset* • *5*

Enhance The crunchy vegetables of a tangy piccalilli do wonders for the crystalline texture of Montgomery Cheddar, with its fine layering and crumbly bite.

Contrast Another West Country gem, Montgomery Cheddar is known for its deeply nutty character, which contrasts with the sharp, piquant veg in piccalilli.

Balance This is a robust, bold cheese, with powerful umami meatiness. The turmeric in piccalilli lends it an earthiness that is well matched, while also bringing sour and sweet notes to the pairing for balance.

STICHELTON & CARAMELIZED WALNUTS

• *Cow's milk* • *Welbeck, Nottinghamshire* • *5*

Enhance Beneath the natural rind of a Stichelton lies a sweet, creamy layer of pale, soft cheese, which is a magnet for the creaminess of walnuts.

Contrast The subtle blue veins in this cheese impart a soft fruitiness to the paste of the cheese. I adore this against the walnuts, which are equally soft in their nutty bite. The contrast is enough to be distinct, but neither is too powerful to overwhelm the other.

Balance Using caramelized walnuts is a great way to bring sweetness to this otherwise sour, bitter, salty and umami pairing (cheese and nuts – what could be more savoury?). That sugar coating is just what it needs to bring a toffee caramel that rounds off each bite.

Try also:
Cornish Kern & espresso martini
Corra Linn & orange quince
Eve goat's cheese & fresh grapes
Perl Las & sultanas
Sinodun Hill goat's cheese & Picpoul wine
Ticklemore & flower honey
Wigmore & raw pear chutney
Winslade & fresh truffles

Bacon jam

This salty-sweet jam with a touch of heat is quick and easy to make, and is incredibly morish. The rich, caramelized flavours make it an ideal pairing for a strong Cheddar. In particular, I like to serve it with Quicke's Vintage Cheddar or Westcombe Cheddar.

MAKES 1 X 300G/10½OZ JAR

500g/1lb 2oz smoked bacon, chopped into small pieces

60g/2oz molasses

60g/2oz light brown soft sugar

1 teaspoon onion powder

¼ teaspoon cayenne pepper, or to taste

¼ teaspoon fine sea salt, or to taste

1 In a large skillet or frying pan, cook the chopped bacon over medium heat until it becomes crispy and the fat is rendered (about 8–10 minutes). Remove the bacon from the pan and set it aside, leaving the bacon grease in the pan.

2 Reduce the heat to low and add the molasses, sugar, onion powder, cayenne pepper and salt to the pan with the bacon grease. Stir well to combine the ingredients.

3 Return the cooked bacon to the pan and stir it into the molasses mixture until evenly coated.

4 Simmer the mixture over low heat, stirring occasionally, for about 45 minutes to 1 hour. The mixture will thicken and become sticky as it cooks. Adjust the heat as needed to prevent burning. Once the bacon jam reaches a thick, jam-like consistency, remove the pan from the heat.

5 Let the bacon jam cool for a few minutes, then transfer it to a food processor. Pulse the mixture a few times until you reach your desired consistency, you can make it chunky or smooth, depending on your preference. Transfer to a sterilised jar or airtight container. It will keep unopened for up to 3 months in the freezer, 2–4 weeks unopened in the fridge, or 1 week once opened.

Apple butter

A delightful accompaniment for cheese, apple butter is a velvety, caramelized spread that perfectly complements the creamy, tangy notes of favourite British cheeses, such as Ogleshield and Anster. I love making my own.

MAKES ABOUT 750G/1LB 10OZ

2kg/4lb 8oz tart and sweet dessert apples (a mixture of Granny Smith and Golden Delicious works well)

250ml/9fl oz (hard) apple cider or apple juice

2 x 10cm/4in cinnamon sticks

½ teaspoon ground cloves

½ teaspoon ground nutmeg

zest and juice of 1 lemon

400g/14oz granulated sugar

1 Peel and core the apples, then cut them into small chunks or slices, removing any seeds or tough parts. Place the apple pieces in a large saucepan or heavy-bottomed casserole. Add the apple cider or juice, cinnamon sticks, cloves, nutmeg, and lemon zest and juice. Bring the mixture to the boil over medium heat, then reduce the heat to low and simmer, stirring occasionally, for about 1 hour, or until the apples become tender and start to break down.

2 Remove the pan from the heat and remove and discard the cinnamon sticks. Using a hand-held stick blender, purée the apple mixture until smooth, taking care not to scald yourself if the hot mixture splatters.

3 Return the puréed mixture to a low heat, then little by little and stirring continuously, add the granulated sugar until it is all in and it has completely dissolved. Let the mixture simmer for another 1–2 hours, occasionally stirring, until it thickens to a smooth and spreadable consistency. Transfer the butter to an airtight container and leave to cool. It will keep in the fridge for up to 2 weeks.

Cheese pairing *for the seasons*

Burrata + steamed asparagus

Gouda + strawberries

Goat's cheese + radish

Camembert + cherries

Feta + watermelon

Goat's curd + roasted beetroot

Ricotta + baby peas

I love spring – the season of renewal and rejuvenation that sees me reaching for the abundance of fresh, spicy and intensely flavourful pairings that only the new growth of the season can bring. A particular favourite for me here is tangy ricotta with the sweetest, butteriest new peas – ideally straight from the pod. I'm sneaking in strawberries here, too – those late-spring jewels of sweet, juicy deliciousness are everything a Gouda needs to draw out the spicy freshness in its own flavour notes.

Spring

GOAT'S CHEESE & RADISH with microgreens
• *Goat's milk* • *Crottin de Chavignol, Chabis or Vermont Creamery fresh goat's cheese* • *2*

Enhance The pepperiness in radish is a great way to enhance the tangy nature of goat's cheese. All my favourites give tang in this pairing, although the Crottin de Chavignol is the most powerful.
Contrast The obvious contrast here is in texture. All my favourites are luxuriously creamy and bounce off the crunch of the radish.
Balance Freshness in radish tempers its spiciness to create perfect balance with the delicately flavoured cheese. The combination gives salty and sour from the cheese and bitter from the bright and bold radish.

RICOTTA & BABY PEAS with lemon zest
• *Various milks* • *Gioiella Rich Ricotta Hearts* • *1*

Enhance Tender, new season peas have a mildly sweet flavour and naturally buttery texture that is heavenly when paired with a fresh and rich ricotta cheese.
Contrast The clean, crisp skin and smooth flesh of the peas form a delightful contrast on the palate against the grainy, soft ricotta. That burst of spring freshness as you bite into the peas floods the ricotta with sweet, tart flavour.
Balance Ricotta (literally meaning 're-cooked') is a gentle and easy-going soft cheese made using the whey by-product of other cheesemaking. Creamy in its nature rather than tangy, it is well-balanced in intensity by the umami-rich, mildly flavoured young peas, which elevate rather than overpower.

FETA & WATERMELON with mint
• *Ewe's milk* • *Graceburn* • *1*

Enhance There's freshness in abundance in this pairing, which sings of spring. A young feta, with a mild flavour is juicy and lively, exactly like a perfect early-season watermelon.
Contrast Feta has a renowned crumbly texture that plays on the tongue in sharp contrast to the crisp, hydrating mouthfeel of watermelon.
Balance A young feta is layered with cream and sour notes, which are balanced with the gentle sweetness and mild anise of the fruit. A more intense sweetness would overpower this delicately flavoured cheese.

BURRATA & STEAMED ASPARAGUS with lemon-infused olive oil
• *Cow's milk* • *Burrata di Bufala* • *1*

Enhance Although burrata is luxuriously creamy and decadent, the fact that its interior is raw, shredded curds mixed with cream gives it a buttery, rich earthiness that works so beautifully with tender, new-season asparagus spears. Together they remind us that fresh flavour comes in many guises.
Contrast I love that the grassy, nutty flavour of asparagus sings against mild and milky burrata. In fact, burrata is generally more flavourful than straight mozzarella (which forms the outside of the burrata ball), but its richness is contrasted well in this pairing.
Balance Asparagus brings a delicate bitterness that is countered by the creamy burrata. Some burrata can have a mild saltiness that rounds off the pairing.

GOUDA & STRAWBERRIES
with balsamic glaze
• Cow's milk • Beemster Young Gouda or Henri Willig • 4

Enhance Late in spring come strawberries, here tempting out the subtle sweetness that lies in the layers of complex Gouda. This is a particular feature of Beemster Young, which is a beautiful pair for the fruit.
Contrast Gouda has a smooth, buttery and firm texture that is in contrast to the fleshy burst of juicy strawberries. The contrast works because one is giving salty tang and the other an explosion of sweetness.
Balance Nuttiness in the Gouda pairs gorgeously with the tangy, sweet fruit for complete harmony.

CAMEMBERT & CHERRIES
with lavender honey
• Cow's milk • Camembert de Normandie AOC • 2

Enhance Camembert de Normandie, as opposed to commercially produced Camembert, has a subtle tanginess that beautifully ripe, springtime cherries draw to the fore with their own tart flavour.
Contrast The burst of tangy cherry fruit is a foil for the creamy, buttery and earthy nature of Camembert, while the cherries' mild liquorice/aniseed flavour balances the voluptuousness of the cheese.
Balance Sweet and sour are defining characteristics of cherry fruit, while cherry stones (which are inedible) impart a slight bitterness into the flesh that helps to temper the sweetness. Camembert brings mushroomy umami in bucket-loads to create a well-rounded pairing on the palate.

GOAT'S CURD & ROASTED BEETROOT (BEETS)
with crushed pistachios
• Goat's milk • White Lake English Goat's Curd • 2

Enhance Roasted beetroot is perfect for tempting out the subtle sweetness and gentle acidity of goat's curd (which is fresher and fluffier than regular goat's cheese).
Contrast Tart and tangy, light and creamy goat's curd contrasts in both flavour and texture to earthy, rooty and dense beetroot. The colour contrast of these two is stunning – this feast for the eyes is as mouthwatering as the first bite.
Balance This is a well-rounded pairing, with the beetroot bringing sweet, mildly spicy and bitter notes, and the complex goat's curd offering sour, lemon notes and a creamy, sumptuous mouthfeel. This is a mild cheese that is well balanced by the muted acidity and abundant caramelized sweetness of the roasted veg.

Try also:
Burrata & roasted baby leeks with olive oil
Chèvre & wild garlic
Chaource & poached apricots with pistachios
Ricotta & fresh oranges with honey
Whipped burrata & roasted beetroot (beets) with grapefruit

Burrata & asparagus pesto pasta

Straight from the spring pairings board, this pasta recipe is the perfect way to welcome the season. The recipe combines the crispness of asparagus, the tanginess of lemon, and the creaminess of burrata cheese, resulting in a dish that is both simple and delicious. I serve this with a pipette full of pesto so you can squeeze and fill the burrata.

SERVES 4

300g/10½oz dried pasta of choice (I like penne, fusilli or rigatoni)

1 tablespoon unsalted butter

1 tablespoon extra-virgin olive oil

250g/9oz asparagus, woody stems discarded, tender spears chopped

1–2 teaspoons chilli flakes (if you like a bit of spice), to taste

150g/5½oz Pecorino Romano, grated, plus extra to serve

1 x 150g/5½oz ball of burrata

zest of ½ lemon

freshly ground black pepper

FOR THE PESTO

30g/1oz basil20g/¾oz rocket (arugula)

2 garlic cloves

50g/1¾oz walnuts

20g/¾oz Pecorino Romano, grated

2–3 tablespoons extra-virgin olive oil

juice of ½ lemon

a generous pinch of sea salt and freshly ground black pepper

1 Bring a large saucepan of salted water to the boil. Add the pasta and cook for 8–10 minutes, or until al dente. Drain, reserving a cup of of the cooking water, and set aside.

2 While the pasta is cooking, make the pesto. Add the pesto ingredients to a blender or mini food processor and pulse until smooth. You may need to loosen the pesto with some water (not more than about 2 tablespoons) to create the desired consistency. This pesto should be a fairly loose paste. Set aside.

3 Melt the butter with the olive oil in a large saucepan over medium heat. Add the chopped asparagus and sauté for about 2 minutes, then add the chilli flakes (if using) and homemade pesto. Stir everything together, and let the flavours combine for a minute or two.

4 Tip the cooked pasta into the pan with the asparagus and pesto and stir to ensure that the pasta is well coated in the sauce. Add the Pecorino Romano and a splash of the reserved starchy pasta cooking water and continue to stir everything for a few minutes, allowing the cheese to melt into the sauce. If the sauce thickens too much, you can add a splash more pasta water to loosen it.

5 Transfer the pasta to a serving dish and top with torn burrata, lemon zest, freshly ground black pepper and more grated Pecorino.

Wine pairing: A light-bodied white wine, such as Pinot Grigio, Sauvignon Blanc or Vermentino would pair nicely. These wines have a crisp acidity that complements the bright and fresh flavours of the asparagus pesto and the creaminess of the burrata cheese.

Camembert, cherry & mixed berry grilled-cheese sandwich

The luscious and creamy texture of Camembert beautifully complements the sweet and tart notes of cherries and berries, which are just coming into flavourful season in late spring. This classic French combination brings together the best of all worlds, creating a perfect balance of creaminess and fruitiness.

MAKES 4

8 slices of your favourite bread (I like sourdough or French baguette), buttered on one side

salted butter, softened, for spreading

1 ripe Camembert (about 250g/9oz), cut into thin slices

150g/5½oz cherries, pitted and halved

150g/5½oz mixed berries (such as strawberries, blueberries and raspberries), sliced or whole

optional additions: rocket (arugula) leaves or prosciutto

runny honey, for drizzling (optional)

1 Preheat a griddle pan over a medium heat.

2 Butter the bread slices on one side and place 4 slices, buttered sides down, on a clean work surface. Layer the Camembert slices equally on top of the 4 slices of bread, top with the cherry halves and mixed berries and add any of your optional additions. Top with the remaining four slices of bread, buttered sides up.

Wine pairing: A Pinot Noir's red fruit flavours, such as cherry and raspberry, complement the fruitiness of the dish while providing a refreshing acidity to balance the richness of the cheese.

3 Carefully transfer two of the sandwiches to the hot griddle pan. Cook for 3–4 minutes on each side, or until the bread is golden brown and the cheese has melted. If you like, drizzle a touch of honey over the sandwiches for extra sweetness.

4 Remove the grilled cheese sandwiches from the griddle. Repeat with the other two sandwiches. Let the sandwiches cool for a minute before cutting them in half and serving.

No-churn honey, lemon, thyme & ricotta ice cream

When it comes to frozen desserts, cheese ice cream might not be the first thing that comes to mind. However, prepare to be pleasantly surprised by the velvety smooth texture and delicious flavours of this frozen delight. Served inside real Sicilian lemons perched on a bed of ice, each one is a feast for the eyes as well as the taste buds. With its vibrant colour and summery aesthetic, this dessert is one of my favourites.

SERVES 6

3 Sicilian lemons

2 tablespoons cornflour (cornstarch)

250ml/9oz whole milk

180ml/6fl oz double (heavy) cream

4–6 thyme sprigs

1 vanilla pod, seeds scraped out (reserve the pod)

4 tablespoons runny honey

2 tablespoons granulated sugar

340g/11¾oz ricotta

3 tablespoons full-fat cream cheese, at room temperature

½ teaspoon flaked sea (kosher) salt

mint leaves, to decorate

1 Halve the lemons lengthways and carefully scoop out the flesh, keeping the lemon shells intact. Transfer the flesh and juice to a bowl, cover with cling film (plastic wrap) and set aside in the fridge.

2 In a small bowl, whisk the cornflour with about 3 tablespoons of the milk to make a smooth slurry.

3 In a small saucepan, bring the remaining milk and the cream to the boil over a medium heat. As soon as it starts to boil, remove from the heat and add the thyme and vanilla pod and seeds. Cover the pan with a lid and leave to infuse for 20 minutes.

4 Strain the milk mixture into a bowl to remove the thyme and vanilla pod. Return the mixture to the saucepan and place over a medium-high heat.

5 Give the cornflour slurry one last whisk, then little by little, whisk it into the milk and cream, bringing the mixture back to the boil. Keep cooking, whisking continuously, until the mixture thickens enough to coat the back of a spoon (about 1 minute).

6 Stir 1 tablespoon of lemon juice, the honey and the sugar into the thickened cream mixture, mixing until they dissolve. Remove from the heat.

7 Pour the mixture into a food processor or blender and add the ricotta, cream cheese and salt. Blitz until completely smooth, then pour into a shallow container and leave to cool. Once cold, put the lid on the container and transfer it to the freezer. Freeze for 1 hour, then remove the lid and stir the mixture (it should be part-frozen) vigorously with a fork to break up any ice crystals. Replace the lid and return to the freezer. Repeat the process, stirring every 30 minutes for 2–3 hours, until the ice cream is smooth, creamy, and firm but scoopable. (You can also churn the ice cream in an ice-cream machine and transfer it to the freezer until ready to serve.)

8 To serve, fill each shell with scoops of ricotta ice cream, then drizzle over some of the reserved lemon juice. You can return the filled lemon shells to the freezer, until you're ready to serve them – just give them 10 minutes at room temperature to soften a little before you do.

Blossom breeze

This light, floral cocktail is the perfect, refreshing drink to toast the arrival of spring. The sweetness of new-season strawberries and the perfumed notes of lavender pair beautifully with zesty, light cheeses such as chèvre and feta.

SERVES 1

2–3 fresh strawberries, quartered

45ml/1½fl oz vodka

30ml/1fl oz lemon juice

22ml/¾fl oz Lavender-infused Simple Syrup (see below)

ice cubes

edible flower, to decorate

FOR THE LAVENDER-INFUSED SIMPLE SYRUP:

200g/7oz granulated sugar

2 tablespoons dried lavender buds

1 To make the simple syrup, combine 235ml/8fl oz water with the sugar and dried lavender buds in a small saucepan. Bring to a boil, stirring until the sugar dissolves. Remove from heat and set aside for 15–20 minutes.

2 Strain the syrup to remove the lavender buds and let the syrup cool completely before using. Pour into a sterilized bottle and store in a cool dark place for up to 2 months.

3 To make the cocktail, in a cocktail shaker muddle the fresh strawberries until they release their juices.

4 Add the vodka, lemon juice, lavender-infused simple syrup, and a handful of ice cubes to the shaker. Shake vigorously for about 15 seconds to combine and chill the ingredients, then strain the cocktail into a chilled glass filled with ice cubes.

5 Garnish with an edible flower then serve the cocktail alongside the Spring Board (see pages 162–165).

Grilled halloumi + roasted pineapple and chilli

Semi-cured manchego + grilled Mediterranean vegetables

Feta + cucumber

Burrata + basil pesto

Goat's cheese + honeycomb

Feta + lemon-roasted courgette

Gouda + watermelon and mint

Light, fresh, bright and zesty – those are the adjectives I like to think of when I gather my summer pairings. Paired with zingy bedfellows, you can bring out the breezier, sunshine notes in even the most rich and earthy cheeses – mint brings instant freshness, balsamic brings warm breezes, and the fresh, herby character of coriander and instant zestiness of citrus simply do their summery thing. Bring on the barbecue!

Summer

SEMI-CURED MANCHEGO & GRILLED MEDITERRANEAN VEGETABLES
with balsamic glaze
• *Cow's milk* • *La Oveja Negra (Semi-Curado)* • *3*

Enhance The softer texture in this cheese compared with other Manchegos is complemented in the soft, grilled vegetables.
Contrast Give a semi-cured Manchego a good sniff and you'll find a citrussy quality on the nose. Opposites attract with the grilled vegetables' smoky intensity.
Balance Sweet in the intensified flavours of the vegetables and bitterness in the blackened skins; sourness and gentle saltiness in the Manchego with its natural umami depth – this is a pairing that gives perfect, all-rounded balance.

FETA & CUCUMBER with mint
• *Ewe & goat's milk* • *Arvaniti Barrel-aged PDO* • *1*

Enhance If any one pairing could speak summer to me, it would be cucumber and feta. Both moist and light, they are each other's homage to freshness.
Contrast Ageing in wooden barrels gives my favourite here a tangy, woody edge (a complexity rarely seen in feta) that is in clear contrast to the crisp cucumber.
Balance I wanted to balance the creamy, light texture of this young feta with cucumber that brings a good, solid crunch, as it overrides any butteriness in the cheese.

GOAT'S CHEESE & HONEYCOMB
with lavender
• *Goat's milk* • *Sainte-Maure de Touraine* • *2*

Enhance The fizz of honeycomb and zesty quality of goat's cheese are given uplift when they are tasted together. It's zing for the senses.
Contrast Fresh goat's cheese has a particularly crumbly texture that contrasts beautifully with the honeycomb's dense, sticky snap. The cheese is sour and lemony against the candy-sweet caramel of the honeycomb.

Balance Choose a young goat's cheese with a light intensity – the bold sweetness of the honeycomb makes sure there is equilibrium on the palate.

GRILLED HALLOUMI & ROASTED PINEAPPLE AND CHILLI
with fresh coriander (cilantro)
• *Goat's milk* • *Maroullas Cypriot 100% Goat's* • *2*

Enhance The mild, creamy flavour of halloumi provides a wonderful canvas for the intensely sweet flavour from the grilled pineapple and the spice from the chilli.
Contrast Halloumi has a characteristic squeaky texture that is in great contrast to the tender slump of grilled pineapple, which gives a burst of juice over the cheese as you take a bite.
Balance Halloumi's saltiness needs the powerful sweetness of the pineapple and the spicy hit from the chilli to make sure there is good balance on the palate.

BURRATA & BASIL PESTO with lemon zest
• *Cow's milk* • *Burrata di Andria PGI* • *1*

Enhance Creamy, indulgent and luxurious, burrata brings out the creamy notes in the pine nuts and Parmesan that make up the pesto.
Contrast Choose a pesto that has some nutty crunch left in it to make sure you offset all that smooth, decadent mouthfeel with something (literally) to get your teeth into. The pliable, mozzarella skin of the burrata gives way to the cream-rich, spun inner.
Balance Burrata is, by definition, super-mild in its cheesy intensity and it welcomes the powerful, herby tanginess of garlic, basil and Parmesan to give it that burst of summer life.

Try also:
Feta & lemon-roasted courgette (zucchini) with toasted pine nuts
Gouda & watermelon with rocket (arugula)

Lemon & feta roasted courgettes

Straight from the spring pairings board, this pasta recipe is the perfect way to welcome the season. The recipe combines the crispness of asparagus, the tanginess of lemon, and the creaminess of burrata cheese, resulting in a dish that is both simple and delicious.

SERVES 4–6 AS A SIDE

3 courgettes (zucchini), halved lengthways

2 garlic cloves, very finely chopped

3 tablespoons extra-virgin olive oil

50g/1¾oz feta cheese, crumbled

1 tablespoon lemon juice

a small handful of basil leaves

sea salt and freshly ground black pepper

1 Preheat the oven to 220°C/200°C fan/425°F/Gas 7.

2 Score the courgette halves by making shallow cuts in a diamond pattern about 3mm/⅛in deep and 5mm/¼in apart – taking care not to cut all the way through. The cuts will help the seasonings penetrate the flesh and create more surface area for browning.

3 In a large bowl, mix together the garlic with 2 tablespoons of the olive oil and season with salt and pepper to taste. Add the scored courgettes to the bowl and toss them gently to coat with the dressing.

4 Arrange the courgettes on a baking sheet, cut sides up, and drizzle them with the remaining olive oil. Roast the courgettes for 20–25 minutes, or until they are tender throughout and golden brown on top.

5 While the courgettes are cooking, mix the crumbled feta cheese with the lemon juice in a small bowl. Once the courgettes are done, remove them from the oven and transfer them to a serving dish. Spoon the feta cheese mixture over the top and sprinkle with the basil to finish.

Wine pairing: This light and refreshing, tangy and savoury dish calls for a dry white wine with high acidity and citrus notes that will complement the flavours nicely. Consider pairing this dish with a Sauvignon Blanc, Pinot Grigio or a dry Riesling.

Orecchiette salad with halloumi

This refreshing dish combines tender orecchiette pasta with warm halloumi cheese, creating a delightful contrast of flavours and textures. Tossed with cherry tomatoes, marinated artichoke hearts and black olives, this salad is brought together with a zesty dressing of fresh lemon juice and fragrant basil.

SERVES 4

300g/10½oz dried orecchiette pasta

4 tablespoons extra-virgin olive oil

225g/8oz halloumi, cut into 5mm/¼in cubes

2 garlic cloves, minced

½–1 teaspoon chilli (hot pepper) flakes, to taste

550g/1lb 4oz cherry tomatoes, halved

120g/4¼oz artichoke hearts in oil, chopped

60g/2oz pitted black olives, sliced

2 tablespoons lemon juice

sea salt and freshly ground black pepper

a large handful basil leaves, torn, to serve

1 Bring a large saucepan of salted water to the boil and cook the orecchiette for a little less time than it states on the packet instructions, until al dente. Drain and set aside.

2 In a large frying pan, heat 2 tablespoons of the olive oil over a medium-high heat. When hot, add the halloumi cubes and cook, turning, until they are golden brown on all sides (about 5 minutes). Remove the halloumi from the pan and set aside.

3 In the same pan, add the remaining olive oil, along with the garlic and chilli flakes. Fry for 1 minute, until fragrant. Add the cherry tomatoes, artichoke hearts and black olives and cook for 3–4 minutes, stirring occasionally, until the tomatoes start to soften and release their juices.

4 Tip the orecchiette into the pan and toss everything together to combine. Cook for 2 minutes to warm the pasta and sauce through, then remove the pan from the heat and drizzle the lemon juice over. Season to taste and toss to combine.

5 Transfer the orecchiette salad to a serving bowl or platter. Top with the crispy halloumi cubes and serve scattered with the torn basil leaves.

Wine pairing: Chardonnay with a moderate level of oak and a good balance of fruit and acidity gives a creamy mouthfeel that works well with the richness of the halloumi cheese, while the acidity enhances the flavours of the cherry tomatoes and lemon juice.

Symphony spritz

I crafted this cocktail to perfectly match the diverse cheese pairings in the Summer board (see pages 174–75), but, in truth, it's delicious at any time of year! With its botanical undertones, vibrant, citrussy zest, and a hint of sweetness, the spritz amplifies the earthiness of Manchego, complements the tanginess of feta, enhances the creaminess of burrata, balances the sharpness of Cheddar, and adds a tantalizing contrast to pairings like halloumi with grilled pineapple and chilli.

SERVES 1

3–4 mint leaves, plus an extra sprig to garnish

2–3 teaspoons lemon juice, to taste

2–3 teaspoons simple syrup, to taste

50ml/1¾fl oz gin

25ml/1fl oz elderflower liqueur

ice cubes

soda water

slice of lemon, to garnish

1 Muddle the fresh mint leaves with the lemon juice and simple syrup in a cocktail shaker until the mint releases its aroma. Add the gin and elderflower liqueur, along with a handful of ice cubes. Pop the lid on the shaker and shake vigorously for about 10–15 seconds to chill the ingredients.

2 Fill a highball? glass with ice cubes and strain the cocktail into the glass. Top up the glass with soda water, leaving some room for your garnish. Stir gently to combine the ingredients, then garnish with the sprig of mint and slice of lemon. Serve immediately, with cheese.

Goat's cheese + roasted butternut squash

Brie + fresh figs

Raclette + boiled baby new potatoes

Camembert + sautéed mushrooms

Cumin Gouda + roasted pumpkin

Époisses or Munster + red apples

Rich, savoury cheeses are the province of autumn, which somehow reflect the golden evening light as summer fades and we prepare for cooler, cozy evenings. Autumn is also a season of great bounty – root vegetables, earthy mushrooms, apples and the second growth of ripe, sweet figs. Summer may be over, but autumn brings so much to enjoy!

Autumn

CUMIN GOUDA & ROASTED PUMPKIN
• *Cow's milk* • *Reypenaer VSOP 2-year aged* • *5*

Enhance I'm using a flavoured Gouda here because cumin ups the ante when it comes to bringing out the nuttiness of the cheese. The pumpkin's naturally nutty, sweet flavour finds its voice here, too.
Contrast I love the 'bite' of the spice in this long-aged, cumin-laced cheese, which gives it a good, strong aroma. Pumpkin, on the other hand, has a heady sweetness that keeps that fragrant strength in check.
Balance Cumin Gouda is earthy, rich and nutty with a sour and spicy kick and is a delight with the sweetness and earthy qualities of pumpkin. Roast the pumpkin sprinkled with rock salt and you'll have an entirely well-rounded and satisfying flavour profile.

GOAT'S CHEESE & ROASTED BUTTERNUT SQUASH
• *Goat's milk* • *Queserias Del Tietar Monte Enebro* • *3*

Enhance Here, we can rely on the roasted butternut squash to bring out the earthy, mineral qualities in the cheese. (An even earthier pairing would be Garrotxa goat's cheese, which is notably woody.)
Contrast Goat's cheese is naturally tangy and my named favourite here is particularly salty and sour on the taste buds. Pair that with creamy, sweet roasted butternut and the contrast creates a flavour explosion.
Balance There's a truly satisfying flavour profile in this pairing – tangy, umami and salty in the cheese with sweet notes from the squash. That balance begins with the aroma and then lingers in the finish – perfect.

CAMEMBERT & SAUTÉED MUSHROOMS
• *Cow's milk* • *Camembert de Normandie AOC* • *1*

Enhance Umami is that 'fifth' taste that makes the other flavours in foods sing. In this pairing, umami comes in abundance – from the earthy mushrooms (the sautéing intensifies their flavour) and deeply savoury Camembert.

Contrast Camembert from the Normandy AOC has a defining creaminess that is hard to replicate. This heady, sumptuous cheese is touched with reality in the forest-floor mushrooms and contrasts beautifully with the strong herbal notes of thyme.
Balance This pairing encapsulates the natural harmony of a woodland meadow – earthy mushrooms and the buttercup creaminess of a mild, soft cheese. Nature gets it so right!

ÉPOISSES OR MUNSTER & RED APPLES
• *Cow's milk* • *Époisses AOP or Munster AOP* • *3*

Enhance These cheeses are bold, strong, pungent, intense and robust – from the minute you remove the packaging! It would be hopeless to try to overpower it in a pairing, so the gently sweet aroma of cut apple simply allows the cheese to sing.
Contrast There's great texture contrast here. This is an oozy, gooey cheese, even though it's young. Apple slices provide a good crunch to offset all that decadence.
Balance There's a risk with these intensely rich cheeses of quickly finding yourself in a cheese stupor – crisp, sweet and juicy apple provides just the right level of balance to keep you coming back for more.

RACLETTE AND BOILED BABY NEW POTATOES
• *Cow's milk* • *Raclette du Valais* • *2*

Enhance A hearty and comforting Swiss tradition for the autumn season, raclette melted over baby new potatoes brings out the butteriness in both.
Contrast Raclettte has a slight tang that contrasts well with the natural flavours of the young potatoes.
Balance Both the cheese and the potatoes bring a creamy, lusciously mild texture and flavour, but this is balanced by the very mild bitterness in the paper-thin skins of new potatoes.

Try also:
Brie & fresh figs

Baked pears with Gorgonzola

Ripe pears stuffed with creamy Gorgonzola cheese is one of the best pairings –
and this amazing dessert even has a 'bridge' in the form of chopped walnuts, too.
Baked to perfection, drizzled with honey and garnished with thyme, this is
altogether a great appetizer for an autumn spread.

SERVES 4

4 ripe pears, halved lengthways

100g/3½oz Gorgonzola, cubed

a handful of chopped walnuts

2 tablespoons salted butter, melted

2 tablespoons runny honey, plus
optional extra to serve

sea salt and freshly ground black
pepper

a few picked thyme leaves, to
sprinkle

1 Preheat your oven to 190°C/170°C
fan/375°F/Gas 5.

2 Using a teaspoon, scoop out and
discard the seeds and core of the
pear halves to create a cavity in each
one. Stuff each pear half with equal
amounts of the cheese, then season
with salt and pepper and top with
chopped walnuts, pressing the
ingredients down lightly to fill the
cavity in each pear.

3 Place the stuffed pear halves in
a baking dish, filled side up, and
drizzle them with the melted butter
and honey.

4 Bake the filled pears for 25–30
minutes, or until the flesh is tender
and the cheese is melted and golden
brown. Remove the pears from the
oven and sprinkle with thyme leaves
and more honey for extra sweetness, if
you like. Serve warm.

Autumn harvest sparkler

This, to me, is the autumn season in a drink – it combines the warm and inviting flavours of spiced rum, apple cider, maple syrup and lemon juice, creating a perfect harmony with the rich and savoury cheeses of the autumn cheese chart. There's no better way to enjoy those cozy nights in.

SERVES 1

ice cubes

50ml/1¾fl oz spiced rum

25ml/1oz (hard) apple cider

1 tablespoon maple syrup

1 tablespoon lemon juice

1 dash of Angostura bitters

soda water

1 cinnamon stick, to decorate

sugar-frosted rosemary sprig, to decorate (see below)

FOR THE SUGAR-FROSTED ROSEMARY SPRIG

2 tablespoons granulated sugar

1 rosemary sprig

1 First, make the sugar-frosted rosemary sprig. Spoon the sugar onto a shallow saucer and set aside. Lightly brush the rosemary sprig with water so that it is moist all over. Dip the sprig into the sugar, turning it to lightly coat the leaves all over. Shake off any excess and set aside to dry while you make the cocktail.

2 Fill a cocktail shaker with the ice. Add the spiced rum, apple cider, maple syrup, lemon juice and Angostura bitters, then pop the lid on the shaker and shake well to combine and chill the ingredients.

3 Fill a highball glass with more ice, and strain the cocktail into the glass. Top up with soda water, stir to gently combine, then decorate with a cinnamon stick and the frosted rosemary sprig, to serve.

Stilton + brandy pickled pears

Fondue + crusted white bread

Brie + caramalized onions

Roquefort + dried cranberries

Cheddar + apple and bacon

Gouda + 70% dark chocolate

I wanted to make my winter pairing board rich with warm and comforting cheese styles and sumptuous, exciting flavours that are delicious to curl up to or perfect for a winter party. There's sumptuous nuttiness from Cheddar and Gouda, reassuring notes from an earthy and creamy brie, the gentle heat of spice from some super-tangy blues, and even a fondue – what could be more warming for friends gathered at a winter table?

Winter

CHEDDAR & APPLE AND BACON
with candied ginger
• *Cow's milk* • *Westcombe Cheddar* • *4*

Enhance Less a pairing and more a trio, this combination celebrates the hearty richness of Cheddar – the bacon, in particular, brings out its saltiness and farmhouse flavours.
Contrast Crunchy apple and chewy bacon feel welcomingly distinct from the creamy, full-bodied texture of the Cheddar.
Balance I've chosen Westcombe Cheddar as my favourite for its particularly wonderful roundness – it gives sweet, sour and salty not just with the first bite but in a characteristically lingering finish. Apple makes sure that sweetness thrives, while the bacon is there for a smoky, salty, long-lasting edge. Yum.

BRIE & CARAMELIZED ONIONS
with the Snowy Sour cocktail
• *Cow's milk* • *Brie de Melun AOC or Moses Sleeper* • *2*

Enhance I'm suggesting a lighter, family-friendly brie for this winter board. Sniff out one with a mushroomy aroma – it will be naturally uplifted against the caramelized onions. Equally, the sourness in the onions picks out a lingering flavour of soured cream in the cheese's decadently buttery finish.
Contrast The particularly creamy texture of a mild brie is contrasted effortlessly by the sweetness of the onions, which cuts through to make sure any milkiness isn't overwhelming.
Balance This is a soft brie, but not a runny, pungent one, which makes it easy to balance against the silky texture in the onions, as well as sweet, bitter and salty flavours. It's simple but gorgeously effective.

STILTON & BRANDY PICKLED PEARS
with pecans
• *Cow's milk* • *Colston Bassett Stilton* • *3*

Enhance The blue mould in Stilton is what gives it its acidity, which is particularly sharp in my favourite from Colston Bassett Stilton. The acidic pickling in the pears is the perfect way to bring this character to the fore. The warm pickling spices are great for picking up the spicy notes in the cheese, too.
Contrast Sour and sweet contrast to optimum effect in this pairing, which is what makes Stilton and pickled pear such an essential on a winter board. Sweetness comes from the pears themselves.
Balance Aroma, finish and texture are all well-balanced here. The cheese has a pungent, aged, old-socks punch that the boozy aroma from the brandy-pickled pears cuts through. There's a salty finish from the cheese, balanced by the sweetness of the fruit, and a creamy, decadent texture that effortlessly melts alongside the silky bite in the pear.

ROQUEFORT & DRIED CRANBERRIES
with toasted hazelnuts
• *Ewe's milk* • *Roquefort AOP* • *3*

Enhance Unlike many other dried fruits, dried cranberries have a particularly sour tang that follows their sweetness. This in turn enhances the zing in an aged Roquefort – the pockets of mould that form in the cheese burst with that triumphantly sharp flavour.
Contrast Roquefort is cage-aged to give it a particularly earthy and complex umami depth. The zing of the cranberries is in sharp contrast with this, providing a light lift for the cheese's bold and dark savouriness.
Balance Moist and soft but crumbly, aged Roquefort is well balanced in texture by the crisp, chewy bite of the dried fruit.

Try also:
Fondue & crusty white bread with apple and honey
Gouda & 70% dark chocolate with candied ginger

Brie & shallot tart

This warm tart makes for a treat on a winter lunchtime, especially if you serve it with a glass of your favourite crisp, white wine in front of a roaring fire. The milder flavour of shallots, here sweetened and caramelized with balsamic vinegar as they bake, make a fantastic savoury choice for the tangy flavour of a brie and the ultimate creaminess of a Délice de Bourgogne.

SERVES 4

8 banana shallots, peeled and halved

2 tablespoons olive oil

2 tablespoons balsamic vinegar

6–8 thyme sprigs, leaves picked, plus extra chopped leaves to garnish

200g/7oz brie, sliced

100g/3½oz Délice de Bourgogne, sliced

1 x 320g/11¼oz sheet of ready-rolled puff pastry

1 egg, beaten

sea salt and freshly ground black pepper

1 Preheat the oven to 180°C/160°C fan/350°F/Gas 4 and line a roughly 24cm x 17cm (9½in x 6½in) baking sheet with baking paper.

2 In a mixing bowl, toss the shallot halves with the olive oil and balsamic vinegar, and season with salt and pepper. Add the thyme leaves and turn the shallots until the leaves are evenly dispersed and the shallots are well coated. Tip the shallots out onto the baking sheet, shuffle them into an even layer and turn them cut side down. Lay the slices of brie and Délice cheese in between and over the top of the shallots, filling in the gaps.

3 On a lightly floured surface, lay out the sheet of puff pastry. Carefully place the pastry sheet over the cheese and shallots in the baking sheet, tucking in the edges slightly. Brush the puff pastry with the beaten egg.

4 Bake the tart in the oven for about 25–30 minutes, or until the puff pastry is crisp and golden brown. Once the tart is out of the oven, leave it to cool for a few minutes, then place a large serving plate or tray over the baking sheet and carefully invert to release the tart onto the plate. Remove the baking paper, if necessary, garnish with chopped thyme leaves and serve warm.

Snowy sour

This cocktail is a great one for Christmas parties and is a beautiful match for the winter cheese pairings – it's warm and comforting profile beautifully complements the distinct characteristics of the cheeses. It enhances the sharpness of Cheddar, balances the creaminess of brie with caramelized onions, and complements the nutty Gouda and spiced nuts. Citrus notes provide a delightful contrast to tangy Stilton paired with pears and walnuts.

SERVES 1

50ml/1¾fl oz Bourbon

25ml/1fl oz lemon juice

20ml/¾fl oz maple syrup

15ml/½fl oz egg white

ice cubes

1 cinnamon stick, to decorate

lemon twist, to decorate

1 Put the Bourbon, lemon juice, maple syrup and egg white into a cocktail shaker. Pop on the lid and give it quick a shake to combine. Remove the lid and add a handful of ice cubes to the shaker, replace the lid and now shake vigorously for 15–20 seconds to fully combine and chill the ingredients, and work up a little froth.

2 Strain the cocktail into a chilled coupé glass or a tumbler filled with ice. Decorate the glass with the cinnamon stick and lemon twist then serve.

200
ULTIMATE
CHEESE
PAIRINGS

FRESH

1. Azeitão DOP (Portugal) & roasted almonds
2. Buffalo mozzarella (Italy) & fresh basil
3. Burrata (Italy) & fresh grilled peaches
4. Caprice des Dieux (France) & beetroot and hazelnuts
5. Feta PDO (Greece) & Kalamata olives
6. Graceburn (England) & walnuts and cavolo nero
7. Mascarpone (Italy) & dark chocolate
8. Quesillo (Queso Oaxaca) (Mexico) & fresh pineapple
9. Ricotta (Italy) & roasted butternut squash
10. Stracchino (Italy) & fresh raspberries
11. Truffeta (Greece) & fresh strawberries

SOFT

12. Ashcombe (England) & hazelnuts
13. Baron Bigod (England) & fresh blackberries
14. Bête-À-Séguin (Canada) & bacon
15. Bluebell Falls Honey & Thyme (Ireland) & lavender honey
16. Brie de Meaux (France) & Beaujolais wine
17. Brie with truffles (France) & Champagne
18. Brillat-Savarin (France) & sloe gin-soaked apples
19. Bruny Island Cheese Co. C2 (Australia) & muña leaf
20. Camembert de Normandie (France) & Champagne
21. Cancoillotte (France) & caviar
22. Carboncino (Italy) & Prosecco DOP
23. Chabichou du Poitou (France) & Sancerre wine
24. Chaource (France) & honey buttered toast
25. Coulommiers (France) & Côtes du Rhône AOC wine
26. Délice de Bourgogne (France) & black truffle, apples and pickled walnut
27. Explorateur (France) & fresh red grapes
28. Harbison (USA) & fig and thyme crackers
29. Humboldt Fog (USA) & fresh figs
30. Idyll (USA) & bacon jam
31. La Sauvagine (Canada) & fresh celery
32. La Tur (Italy) & Asti Spumante
33. Le Goustal la Bergère (France) & briny olives

34. Mahón (Spain) & fresh watermelon
35. Mont D'Or AOP (France) & garlic roasted potatoes
36. Morbier (France) & fresh plums
37. Morro Azul (Brazil) & fresh baguette
38. Neufchâtel AOP (France) & tart cherry compôte
39. Olavidia (Spain) & fresh Muscat grapes
40. Reblochon Fermier (France) & roasted mushrooms
41. Robiola Bosina (Italy) & Chenin Blanc wine
42. Rocamadour AOP (France) & walnut halves
43. Saint-André (France) & salted caramel sauce
44. Saint-Félicien (France) & caramelized onions
45. Saint-Marcellin (France) & fresh oranges
46. Sinodun Hill (England) & rye and charcoal sourdough crackers
47. Somerset Brie (England) & cider jelly
48. St Jude (England) & fresh figs
49. Templier (France) & Provence rosé wine
50. Tomme D'Aydius (France) & fresh cherries
51. Torta de Barros (Spain) & membrillo
52. Tunworth (England) & fresh apples
53. Valençay Chèvre (France) & Chenin Blanc wine
54. Waterloo (England) & light pinot noir wine
55. Wigmore (England) & pear chutney
56. Zimbro (Portugal) & marmelada (Portuguese quince paste)
57. Zingerman's Little Napoleon (USA) & olive oil drizzle
58. Zingerman's Manchester (USA) & pickled onions

SEMI HARD

59. Beecher's Flagship Reserve (USA) & artisan bread
60. Chällerhocker (Switzerland) & French onion confit
61. Cornerstone (England) & pecans
62. Crottin de Chavignol AOP (France) & roasted pears
63. Crottin de Pays (France) & pistachios
64. Innes Log (Scotland) & fresh raspberries
65. Ogleshield (England) & caramelized figs
66. Raclette (Switzerland) & steamed asparagus

67. Saint-Nectaire AOP (France) & roasted apples
68. Taleggio DOP (Italy) & roasted grapes
69. Ticklemore (England) & Beaujolais wine
70. Vacherin Fribourgeois (Switzerland) & steamed baby potatoes
71. Appalachian (USA) & candied radishes
72. Baliehof Houtlandse Asche kaas (Belgium) & roasted cauliflower
73. Deichkäse Edel (Germany) & caramelized almonds
74. Deichkäse Gold (Germany) & roasted Jerusalem artichokes
75. Humble (USA) & sausages
76. Pirano Buffalo (Italy) & courgette flowers
77. Quina (Brazil) & fresh pears

HARD

78. Anster (Scotland) & dippy egg
79. Appleby's Cheshire (England) & fruit cake
80. Alp Blossom (Germany) & Gewürztraminer wine
81. Asiago DOP (Italy) & Chianti wine
82. Beaufort (France) & prosciutto
83. BellaVitano Gold (USA) & hoppy pilsner
84. Blackmount (Scotland) & smoked salmon
85. Black Bomber Cheddar (Wales) & tomato and vodka chutney
86. Cantal AOP (France) & Châteauneuf-du-pape AOC wine
87. Castelmagno DOP (Italy) & chestnut honey
88. Cato Corner Farm Bloomsday (USA) & spicy salami
89. Cave-aged Emmental (Switzerland) & roast beef
90. Colby (USA) & rye bread
91. Comté (France) & fresh cherries
92. Cornish Kern (England) & rye crackers
93. Cornish Yarg (England) & fresh cucumber
94. Esrom (Denmark) & fresh pineapple
95. Etorki (France) & sesame crackers
96. Fiore Sardo (Italy) & fresh oranges
97. Garrotxa (Spain) & fresh blackberries
98. Gouda (Netherlands) & fresh peaches
99. Grafton Village 2-year-aged Cheddar (USA) & Cabernet Sauvignon wine
100. Gruyère (Switzerland) & Amarena cherries
101. Holy Goat La Luna (Australia) & fig jam

102. Havarti (Denmark) & fresh strawberries
103. Idiazabal (Spain) & almonds
104. Isle of Mull (Scotland) & roast beef
105. Jarlsberg (Norway) & Riesling Spätlese wine
106. Keen's Cheddar (England) & crushed coffee beans and honey
107. Kirkham's Lancashire (England) & piccalilli
108. L'Etivaz (Switzerland) & fresh cherries
109. Lancashire Bomb (England) & dill pickled cucumber
110. Lincolnshire Poacher (England) & pilsner
111. Manchego (Spain) & membrillo
112. Mimolette (France) & fresh cantaloupe melon
113. Ossau-Iraty (France) & Cabernet Sauvignon wine
114. Oka (Canada) & dried cranberries
115. Parmigiano-Reggiano (Italy) & balsamic vinegar and strawberries
116. Pecorino Romano (Italy) & fresh cantaloupe melon
117. Provolone Valpadana (Italy) & salami
118. Pyrenees Brebis (France) & Grenache wine
119. Rosemary Manchego (Spain) & Rioja wine
120. São Jorge 4 months PDO (Portugal) & port
121. Sonoma Dry Jack (USA) & dried apricots
122. Sparkenhoe Red Leicester (England) & tomato chutney
123. Tête de Moine (France) & cashew butter and pickled mustard
124. Tetilla (Spain) & fresh strawberries
125. Toma Walser (Italy) & grilled peaches
126. Tomme Crayeuse (France) & fresh plums
127. Tomme de Savoie (France) & roasted beetroot (beets)
128. Truffled Pecorino (Italy) & toasted hazelnuts
129. Ubriaco (Italy) & Robiola Rocchetta
130. Västerbottensost (Sweden) & Gewürztraminer wine
131. Wensleydale with Cranberries (England) & fresh strawberries
132. Westcombe Cheddar (England) & pickled beetroot (beets)
133. Yorkshire Wensleydale (England) & gingerbread
134. Zamorano (Spain) & almonds
135. Aletsch Grand Cru (Switzerland) & marinated globe artichokes

136. Allerdale (England) & watercress
137. Boerengeitenkaas Naturel (Netherlands) & dried rose hip
138. Coolea (Ireland) & caramelized parsnip
139. Eberle Würzig Seit 5 Generationen (Switzerland) & burnt leaks
140. Eleftheria (India) & black coffee
141. Emmentaler AOP Premier Cru (Switzerland) & dried apricots
142. Griffin (USA) & pickled fennel
143. Hafod (England) & truffle butter
144. Kolan Ekstra Stari (Croatia) & pan-fried shallots
145. Konark (India) & mixed berries
146. Lucky Linda Clothbound Cheddar (USA) & apple butter
147. Michel (Germany) & quince and apple preserve
148. Mount Leinster Clothbound Cheddar (Ireland) & orange and whiskey marmalade
149. Müller-Thurgau Rezent (Switzerland) & cumin
150. Nidelven Blå (Norway) & pickled red cabbage
151. Old Amsterdam Goat (Netherlands) & king oyster mushrooms
152. Pilisi 9-months-old (Hungary) & white asparagus
153. Pitchfork Cheddar (England) & spring onion
154. Rouveens Glory Goat (Netherlands) & dried aged beef
155. São Jorge PDO 4 Months (Portugal) & blackcurrant jam
156. Section28 La Saracca (Australia) & hazelnuts

BLUE

157. Bayley Hazen Blue (USA) & honeycomb
158. Beauvale (England) & Somerset ice cider
159. Billy Blue (USA) & fresh cherries
160. Bleu d'Auvergne (France) & fresh pears
161. Blu di Bufala (Italy) & Pinot Grigio wine
162. Cabrales (Spain) & Marcona almonds
163. Cashel Blue Grand Reserve (Ireland) & dark chocolate
164. Colston Bassett Stilton (England) & fresh pears
165. Cornish Blue (England) & dark chocolate brownie

166. Danablu (Denmark) & fresh strawberries
167. Dunbarton Blue (USA) & walnut bread
168. Fourme d'Ambert AOP (France) & spiced honey
169. Gamonéu DOP (Spain) & black cherry compôte
170. Gorgonzola (Italy) & toasted walnuts
171. Harbourne Blue (England) & heather honey
172 Kraftkar (Norway) & rye crackers
173. Lanark Blue (Scotland) & dark chocolate
174. Long Clawson Dairy Blue Stilton (England) & fresh pears
175. Montagnolo Affine (Germany) & caramelized pears
176. Rogue River Blue (USA) & fig brûlée
177. Roquefort AOP (France) & Sauternes wine
178. Saint Agur (France) & fresh pears
179. Shropshire Blue (England) & fresh oranges
180. Stichelton (England) & toasted pecans
181. Valdeón (Spain) & Ribera del Duero wine
182. Buffalo Pirano (Italy) & chestnut honey
183. Devon Blue (England) & fresh blueberries
184. Fior d'Arancio DOCG (Italy) & Picolit wine
185. Kraftkar 7 months (Norway) & fresh sage
186. Krüger Blue (Canada) & fresh peaches
187. Lamucca di Castagno (Italy) & chestnut honey

WASHED RIND

188. Abbaye de Belloc (France) & fresh figs
189. Époisses de Bourgogne (France) & saucisson sec
190. Grayson (USA) & pickled okra
191. Grès des Vosges (France) & saucisson sec
192. Gubbeen (Ireland) & smoked almonds
193. Langres (France) & fresh apricots
194. Livarot (France) & fresh apples
195. Maroilles (France) & pickled onions
196. Munster (France) & fresh apricots
197. Solglad (Norway) & roasted garlic
198. St James (England) & blackberry preserve
199. Stinking Bishop (England) & fresh apples
200. Trou du Cru (France) & Marc de Bourgogne eau de vie

Index

Appenzeller & spiced honey mustard 92
Apple Butter 158
apricots
  Baked Camembert with Apricots 48
artichokes
  Baked Artichokes with Pecorino 44
Asiago & roasted red peppers with
  toasted pine nuts 39
asparagus
  Burrata & Asparagus Pesto Pasta 166
autumn cheese pairings 183–186

Bacon Jam 156
bakery and cheese 53–58
Baron Bigod & blackcurrant jelly 153
Beauvale & dragonfruit 47
beer and cheese 109
  Beery Cheese Dip 110
bloomy cheeses 13
blue cheeses 13
  blue cheese & espresso 121
  blue cheese & oatcakes with
    walnuts 26
  blue cheese & pear jam 92
  blue cheese & pear, orange & ginger
    chutney 92
  blue cheese & pickled red onions
    with candied pecans 65
  blue cheese & stout with honey 109
  blue cheese & truffle honey 85
  blue Stilton & port with dark
    chocolate-dipped figs 102
  Cabrales & walnuts 133
  extra-mature blue cheese &
    pistachios 61
  pairings 199
  Rogue River Blue & fig paste with
    crushed walnuts 147
brandy
  White Wine and Brandy Poached
    Pears 150
brie
  brie & baguette with dessert pear 26
  brie & baguette with red grapes 53

brie & cappucino 121
brie & caramelized onions 189
brie & Champagne with
  strawberries 101
brie & croissant with fig jam 54
brie & French 75 115
brie & fresh figs 183
brie & honey 127
brie & pickled pearl onions 65
Brie & Shallot Tart 190
brie & walnuts 61
brie & white grapes 47
double-cream brie & Belgian
  Tripel with honeycomb 109
British cheese pairings 153–154
burrata
  Burrata & Asparagus Pesto Pasta 166
  burrata & basil pesto with lemon
    zest 175
  burrata & prosciutto 139
  burrata & steamed asparagus with
    lemon-infused olive oil 163
  Burrata Crunchy Croissant 56
  Heaven-sent Burrata, Prosciutto
    & Cherry Tomato Salad 34

Cabrales & walnuts 133
Cacio e Pepe 140
CaerphillyGorwydd Caerphilly &
  Welsh cakes with fresh mint 153–154
Camembert
  Baked Camembert with Apricots 48
  Camembert & cherries with lavender
    honey 164
  Camembert & hazelnut dark
    chocolate with toasted baguette 79
  Camembert & hazelnuts 61
  Camembert & hot honey 85
  Camembert & raspberry jam 91
  Camembert & sautéed mushrooms 183
  Camembert AOC & saison with red
    grapes 109
  Camembert, Cherry and Mixed Berry
    Grilled-cheese Sandwich 168

canapés
  Confit Potato and Cream Cheese
    Canapés 104
  Fancy Goat Curd Canapés 40
Caramel and Herby Popcorn 148
carrots
  Spicy Pickled Carrots
  The Best Roasted Carrots 42
Cashew Nut Brittle 62
Cauliflower, Pickled 68
charcuterie and cheese 33
  Heaven-sent Burrata, Prosciutto
    & Cherry Tomato Salad 34
  Tortilla with Vintage Manchego
    and Chorizo 36
Cheddar
  Cabot Clothbound Cheddar &
    caramel and herby popcorn 147
  Cheddar & almonds 61
  Cheddar & apple bacon with
    candied ginger 189
  Cheddar & black coffee 121
  Cheddar & English breakfast tea 121
  Cheddar & fruit toast with red
    grapes 29
  Cheddar & IPA with multigrain
    crackers 109
  Cheddar & milk chocolate-coated
    nuts with dried cranberries 79
  Cheddar & piccalilli 92
  Cheddar & pickled carrots with
    toasted walnuts 65
  Cheddar & pineapple 47
  Cheddar & sweet & spicy pickles
    with crusty wholegrain bread 65
  Cheddar & Whisky Sour 115
  Cheddar & wholewheat sourdough
    with wholegrain mustard 53
  Montgomery Cheddar & piccalilli 154
cheese 11
  find your inner fromager 18–19
  flavour chart 1215
  how do we taste?

cheese pairing 7–9
  how to use the charts 22
  pair like a pro 20
  steps to pairing 21
  200 ultimate cheese pairings 196–199
cherries
  Camembert, Cherry and Mixed
    Berry Grilled-cheese Sandwich 168
  Cherry Compôte 94
Cheshire
  Appleby's Cheshire & rhubarb
    compôte 153
chocolate and cheese 79–82
  Chocolate Salami 80
  Colombian Hot Chocolate with
    Gooey Cheese 82
  Homemade Chocolate Digestives 76
chorizo
  Tortilla with Vintage Manchego
    and Chorizo 36
chutneys and cheese 91–92
Cider Mac 'n' Cheese 112
cocktails and cheese 115
  Autumn Harvest Sparkler 186
  Blossom Breeze 172
  Citrus Mint Spritzer 118
  Parmesan Espresso Martini 116
  Sparkling Apple Ginger Fizz 118
  Symphony Spritz 180
  The Snowy Sour 192
coffee and cheese 121
  Coffee Cake with Cream-cheese
    Icing 122
Comté & crackers with dried apricots 29
Comté & fig jam 127
Courgettes, Lemon & Feta Roasted 176
crackers and cheese 26–29, 71–76
  Homemade Chocolate Digestives 76
  Rosemary Olive Oil Crackers 74
cream cheese
  Coffee Cake with Cream-cheese
    Icing 122
  Confit Potato and Cream Cheese
    Canapés 104

cream cheese & pumpernickel with
  fresh dill 54

Earl Grey Lincolnshire Plum Bread 58
Époisses & Pinot Noir 101
Époisses & red apples 183
Époisses Fondue with Wine 106

Fennel, Pickled 66
feta
  Baked Feta Filo with Watermelon 50
  feta & cucumber with mint 175
  feta & Kalamata olives 65
  feta & lemon-roasted courgettes
    with toasted pine nuts 175
  feta & watermelon 47
  feta & watermelon with mint 163
  Lemon & Feta roasted Courgettes 176
Fiery Hot Honey 88
figs
  Fig Brûlée 130
  Fig Jam 96
  Spanish Fig Cake 134
fondue & crusty white bead and
  apple with honey 189
Fontina & mushrooms 139
Fontina & sugar snap peas with
  lemon zest 39
French cheese pairings 127
fresh cheeses 12
  brined fresh cheeses 12
  pairings 196
fruit and cheese 47
  Baked Camembert with Apricots 48
  Baked Feta Filo with Watermelon 50
fruit, dried
  Earl Grey Lincolnshire Plum Bread 58
Fudge, Brown 128

Gjetost & Norwegian coffee 121
goat's cheese
  Chèvre & Grüner Veltliner with
    toasted almonds 102
  Chèvre & lavender honey 85, 92

Chèvre & roasted confit garlic 127
Fancy Goat Curd Canapés 40
goat's cheese & cashews 61
goat's cheese & charcoal crackers
  with fresh figs 29
goat's cheese & classic flatbread
  crackers with grilled portobello
  mushrooms & sage 71
goat's cheese & fig jam 92
goat's cheese & fresh figs 47
goat's cheese & fruit toast with
  roasted peach 72
goat's cheese & green tea 121
goat's cheese & honeycomb 85
goat's cheese & honeycomb with
  lavender 175
goat's cheese & radish with
  microgreens 163
goat's cheese & roasted beetroot
  with candied pecans 39
goat's cheese & roasted butternut
  squash 183
goat's cheese & rosemary focaccia
  with balsamic glaze 53
goat's cheese & Serrano ham with
  rocket 33
goat's cheese & white chocolate
  with fresh figs 79
goat's curd & roasted beetroot with
  crushed pistachios 164
Humboldt Fog goat's cheese &
  pickled pears with honey 147
Gorgonzola
  Baked Pears with Gorgonzola 184
  Gorgonzola & Negroni 115
  Gorgonzola & roasted cauliflower
    with fresh thyme leaves 39
  Gorgonzola dolce & Moscato
    d'Asti with pear 102
  Gorgonzola dolce & acacia honey 85
  Gorgonzola dolce & pear 139
  Gorgonzola dolce & pickled radishes
    with rocket 65

Gorgonzola piccante & Belgian
   Dubhel with candied pecans 109
Gorgonzola piccante & papaya 47
Prosciutto & Peach Sandwich with
   Gorgonzola Butter 144
Gouda
   cumin Gouda & roasted pumpkin 183
   Gouda & 70% dark chocolate
      with candied ginger 189
   Gouda & amber ale with 70%
      dark chocolate 109
   Gouda & blueberries 47
   Gouda & dark roast coffee 121
   Gouda & German salami with
      wholegrain mustard 33
   Gouda & honeybee pollen 85
   Gouda & multigrain crackers
      with cranberry chutney 72
   Gouda & roasted carrots with
      honey 39
   Gouda & Seville orange marmalade 91
   Gouda & sourdough with
      caramelized onions 53
   Gouda & strawberries with
      balsamic glaze 163–164
   Gouda & watermelon and mint
      with rocket 175
   Gouda with cumin & walnuts 61
Gruyère & dark chocolate digestives
   with apple 72
Gruyère & Pinot Noir with apple 102
Gruyère & tomato jam 91

halloumi
   grilled halloumi & roasted pineapple
      and chilli with coriander leaf 175
   halloumi & apricot jam 91
   Orecchiette Salad with Halloumi 178
hard cheeses 15
   pairings 197–199
herbs
   Caramel and Herby Popcorn 148
honey and cheese 85
   Easy Homemade Honeycomb 86

Fiery Hot Honey 88
No-churn Honey, Lemon & Ricotta
   Ice Cream 170

Ice Cream, No-churn Honey, Lemon
   & Ricotta 170
Idiazabal & chorizo 133
Italian cheese pairings 139

jams and cheese 91–92
   Cherry Compôte 94
   Fig Jam 96

lemons
   Lemon & Feta roasted Courgettes 176
   No-churn Honey, Lemon & Ricotta
      Ice Cream 170

Manchego
   Manchego & chorizo with
      Marcona almonds 33
   Manchego & red Rioja with
      chorizo 102
   Manchego & rye crackers with
      membrillo 29
   Manchego & sea salt 70% dark
      chocolate with Marcona almonds 79
   Manchego & Serrano ham 133
   semi-cured Manchego & grilled
      Mediterranean vegetables 175
   Tortilla with Vintage Manchego
      and Chorizo 36
Monte Enebro & rosemary crackers 133
mozzarella
   buffalo mozzarella & Aperol Spritz 115
   buffalo mozzarella & Pilsner with
      cherry tomatoes 109
   buffalo mozzarella & taralli
      with roasted cherry tomatoes 71
   Colombian Hot Chocolate with
      Gooey Cheese 82
   mozzarella & tomato 139
   My Beautiful Bruschette 142
Munster & red apples 183

nuts and cheese 61
   Cashew Nut Brittle 62

Ogleshield & smoky bacon 154
olives and cheese 65
   feta & Kalamata olives 65
onions
   Brie & Shallot Tart 190
   Pickled Red Onions 68
Orange Membrillo 136

Parmesan
   Parmesan & balsamic vinegar 139
   Parmesan & ciabatta with fresh
      basil 53
   Parmesan & dark chocolate
      orange with candied peel 79
   Parmesan & hazelnuts 61
   Parmesan & mango 47
   Parmesan & radicchio with
      balsamic glaze 39
   Parmesan Espresso Martini 116
pasta
   Burrata & Asparagus Pesto Pasta 166
   Cacio e Pepe 140
   Cider Mac 'n' Cheese 112
   Orecchiette Salad with Halloumi 178
peaches
   Prosciutto & Peach Sandwich
      with Gorgonzola Butter 144
pears
   Baked Pears with Gorgonzola 184
   White Wine and Brandy Poached
      Pears 150
Pecorino
   Baked Artichokes with Pecorino 44
   Cacio e Pepe 140
   Pecorino & damson fruit paste 92
   Pecorino Romano & bresaola
      with lemon zest 33
   Pecorino Romano & rosemary
      crackers with truffle oil 72
   Pecorino Toscano & broad beans 139

Pecorino Toscano & Sangiovese
   with cherry jam 101
pesto
   Burrata & Asparagus Pesto Pasta 166
   My Beautiful Bruschette 142
pickles and cheese 65–68
popcorn
   Caramel and Herby Popcorn 148
potatoes
   Confit Potato and Cream Cheese
      Canapés 104
prosciutto
   Heaven-sent Burrata, Prosciutto
      & Cherry Tomato Salad 34
   Prosciutto & Peach Sandwich
      with Gorgonzola Butter 144

quinces
   Orange Membrillo 136

raclette and boiled baby new
   potatoes 183
ricotta
   No-churn Honey, Lemon & Ricotta
      Ice Cream 170
   ricotta & baby peas with lemon
      zest 163
   ricotta & strawberries 47
Rogue River Blue & fig paste
   with crushed walnuts 147
Roquefort
   Roquefort & chilli 70% dark
      chocolate with honey 79
   Roquefort & dried cranberries
      with toasted hazelnuts 189
   Roquefort & nut brittle 61
   Roquefort & rye crackers with
      caramelized onions 71
   Roquefort & saucisson sec with
      fresh figs 33
   Roquefort & Sauternes with
      honeycomb 101
   Roquefort & walnuts 127
Rosemary Olive Oil Crackers 74

Rush Creek Reserve & warm
   crusty bread with truffle oil 147

Saint-Nectaire & bitter with salted
   nuts 109
semi hard cheeses 14
   pairings 197
soft cheeses
   creamy soft cheese & charcoal
      crackers with truffle honey 71
   pairings 196–197
   soft cheese & chilli jam 91–92
   soft cheese & milk chocolate
      with caramel drizzle 79
Spanish cheese pairings 133
spring cheese pairings 163–172
Stichelton & caramelized walnuts 154
Stilton
   blue Stilton & port with dark
      chocolate-dipped figs 102
   Stilton & brandy pickled pears
      with walnuts 189
   Stilton & Jamón Ibérico with
      membrillo 33
Stinking Bishop & caramelized
   onion chutney 153
summer cheese pairings 175–180
Swiss Cheese & Gin Martini 115
Swiss cheese & macadamias 61
Swiss cheese & mocha 121
Swiss cheese & pickled cauliflower
   with roasted red peppers 65

Taleggio & chestnut honey 85
tea and cheese 121
   Earl Grey Lincolnshire Plum Bread 58
tetilla & Spanish honey 133
tomatoes
   Heaven-sent Burrata, Prosciutto
      & Cherry Tomato Salad 34
   My Beautiful Bruschette 142
Tomme de Savoie & apricot jam 127
Torta de Barros & membrillo 133

Tortilla with Vintage Manchego and
   Chorizo 36
triple cream & plum chutney 92
Tunworth & smoked salmon 153

US cheese pairings 147–148

vegetables and cheese 39
   Baked Artichokes with Pecorino 44
   Fancy Goat Curd Canapés 40
   The Best Roasted Carrots 42

washed rind cheeses 14
watermelon
   Baked Feta Filo with Watermelon 50
Wensleydale & Lancashire plum
   bread with spiced apple chutney 54
wine and cheese 101–102
   Époisses Fondue with Wine 106
   White Wine and Brandy Poached
      Pears 150
winter cheese pairings 189–192

Acknowledgements

To my amazingly wonderful family and friends, who are a sounding board for ideas, cheese tasters and spell checkers. How lucky I am to have the best possible people around me. And of course Nelly, Chief Cheese Consultant!

Mum and Dad: I've said it before and I'll say it again, I would not be here without you supporting everything I do without question. Dad: thank you for looking after the cheese shop when I was writing and pregnant, and Mum, thank you for helping me with Georgie, I'm so lucky to have you. I love you both so much.

George and Cicely: I lucked out when it comes to you two. Even though you have zero interest in cheese, you have always pretended to be interested when I talk about it! Love you.

Ben: thank you for being the most supportive, kind, beautiful person who cheers me on whatever I do. I'm so lucky to be able to call you my husband. I love you beyond words.

Jessica: thank you for always believing in me and helping me bring my ideas into reality. And for always being a huge support, especially this time with Georgie in my belly.

Jamie: we both know I wouldn't be on my third book if it wasn't for you. Photographer, food stylist, sous chef and cheerleader. Book number three, go us!!! Bring on the next three lol.

Charlotte: thank you soooo much for being an incredible support throughout this book, from the shoot to the text and everything in between. I wouldn't have been able to do it without you.

Judy: I know that you went above and beyond to help with the book and I will forever be grateful. You are fabulous! Thank you for taking the ramblings of a heavily pregnant women and making sense of it all.

Freya: everything you touch becomes beautiful! Thank you for everything: the hours of making my recipes look fabulous and making fruit look like art. And thank you for lending me your Home Alone grill hook, which will forever be my favourite kitchen tool.

Hannah: thank you so much for making sure we had the most stunning foundations and canvases for the cheeses, and helping me make this book look so pretty.

And to all the Quarto & White Lion publishing team for the continued support for this book and the two before.

Tim, Simon, Charlie, Paddy and all my Sunday Brunch family: thank you for always being so loving and supportive, and giving me a platform to tell everyone about the cheeses I love.

Thank you to the amazing cheesemakers, farmers, affineurs and suppliers from across the world. Your craft, history and stories are the reason I love cheese so much. To all the other cheesemongers out there, your sharing of knowledge, expertise and guidance keeps the cheese world going round. Lastly, thank you to all of the cheese lovers that support, like and share my work. I'm forever grateful.

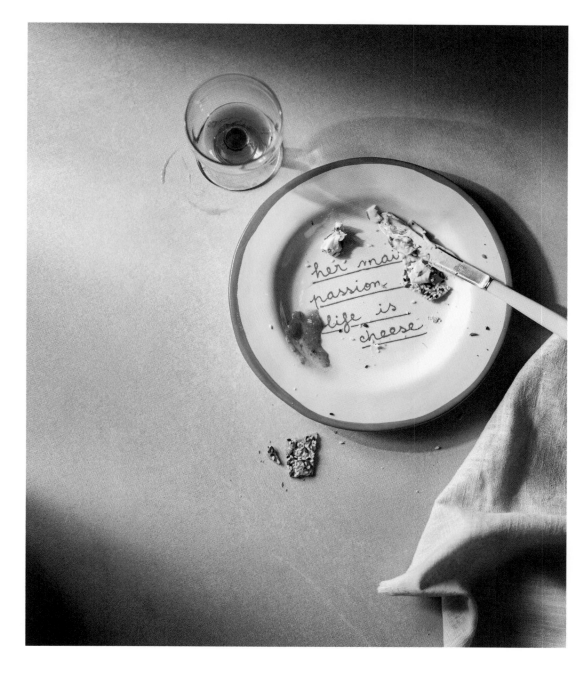

Quarto

First published in 2024 by White Lion Publishing
an imprint of The Quarto Group.
One Triptych Place, London, SE1 9SH
United Kingdom
T (0)20 7700 6700
www.Quarto.com

A catalogue record for this book is available from the British
Library.

ISBN 978-0-7112-9094-5
EBOOK ISBN 978-0-7112-9320-5

10 9 8 7 6 5 4 3 2 1

Book Designer Claire Rochford
Editor Charlotte Frost
Editorial Director Nicky Hill
Food Stylist Freya Matchett
Photographer Jamie Orlando Smith
Prop Stylist Hannah Wilkinson
Project Editor Judy Barratt
Publisher Jessica Axe
Senior Designer Renata Latipova
Senior Production Controller Rohana Yusof

Printed in Slovenia by GPS Group

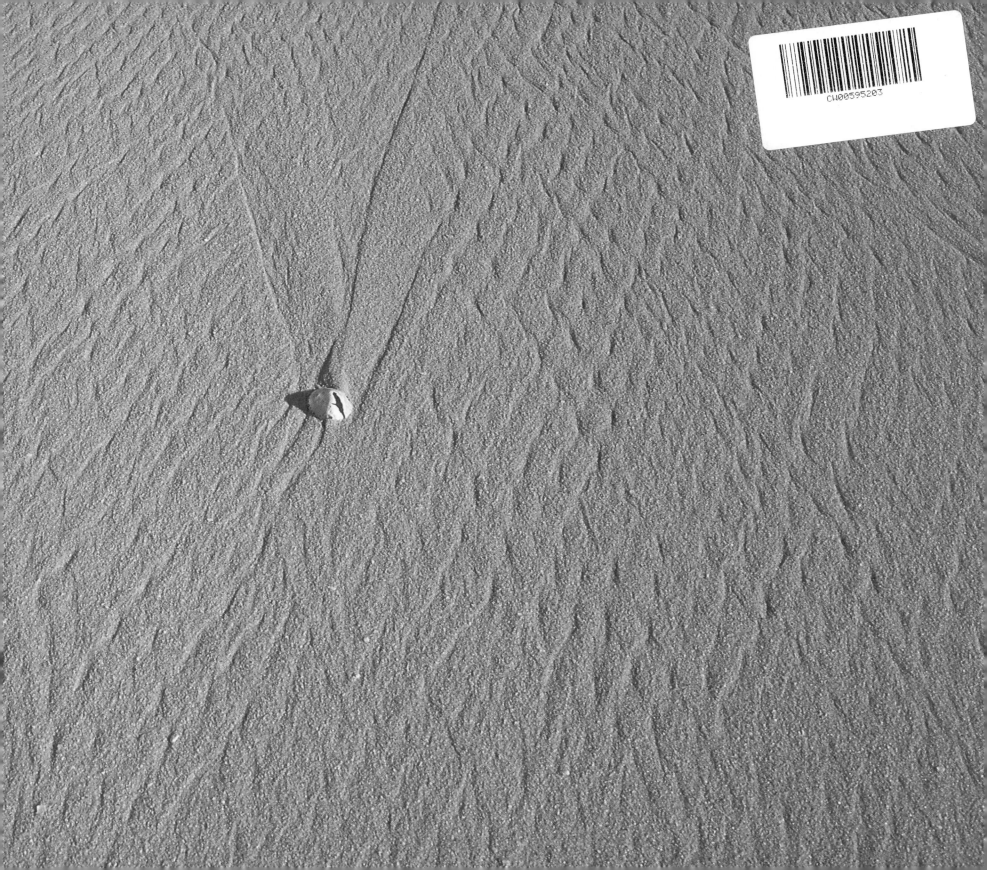

AUSTRALIA'S BIGGEST

WESTERN AUSTRALIA

Photography by
Greg Hocking

First Published 1999
By Design by Nature Press
7 Aries Court Shelley WA 6148
Telephone 08 9457 0342
Email:altitude@ozemail.com.au

ISBN 0 646 37891 0.

National Library of Australia
Cataloguing-in-Publication data.

Hocking, Greg, 1955-.
"Australia's biggest" Western Australia.

Includes index.
ISBN 0 646 37891 0.

Western Australia - Pictorial works. 1. Title.
919.4100222

EDITOR: Greg Hocking *M.PHOTOG.*
DESIGN: Jude Hendricks
           COMPLETE IMAGING CENTRE

PRE-PRESS:

PRINTED BY:

Photograph by Des Birt

GREG HOCKING is one of Australia's leading landscape and scenic photographers having won the *Western Australian Landscape Photographer Award* in 1996 and 1998 as well as the *AIPP Australian Landscape Photographer of the Year Award* in 1997 and 1999. Greg is also a Double Master of Photography with the Australian Institute of Professional Photography. He is renowned for his black and white limited edition photography, which has been collected and exhibited in the UK and America. In Australia's Biggest, Greg has concentrated on the medium of colour to portray the beauty and diverse panorama of Australia's biggest State, Western Australia. This is Greg's first book and celebrates the vast size and unique beauty of the State he calls home.

ACKNOWLEDGEMENTS

The essence of this book may appear to be a personal and solo endeavour but this has been far from the case. The book is linked in various and important ways to these individuals. For their help and support I am grateful.

Di Evans, who, when words failed me, came forward to express in words what my photographs were saying visually.

Malcolm McDonald of Custom Colour Laboratories for the generous support in providing E6 processing for the book.

Lyn Whitfield-King for writing her kind and thoughtful foreword in the front of this book.

Des Birt, a steady friend with a clear light for the path.

A special mentions for Roger Garwood, Trish Ainslie and Richard Woldendorp for the generous advice and guidance on book publishing.

Barry Evans for his great enthusiasm and assistance in the attainment of this book project.

To my family, Janet, Merise, Bethany and Rosalie Hocking, their love and support has driven me on to realize a dream.

AUSTRALIA'S BIGGEST

WESTERN AUSTRALIA

DESIGN BY
NATURE
PRESS

Photography by
Greg Hocking

INTRODUCTION

At 2,527,252 square kilometers in area, Western Australia is Australia's biggest State. Its sheer size is very evident when travelling Western Australia's roads or flying over its diverse and ancient terrain. Western Australia is a rich State; its wealth exists in its scenic beauty, its natural resources and people. Australia's Western third also supports a broad range of agricultural products and industries, many of which are practiced on a grand scale. The West has a diverse range of ethnic and cultural groups, all of which are immensely proud of their State's achievements whether social, commercial, or on the sporting field.

The first inhabitants of the region were the aboriginal people who migrated to Australia from Asia over 40,000 years ago. The Aboriginal people have a strong link to the land, which is an integral part of their cultural and physical existence. Recorded history shows that Europeans first visited Western Australia nearly 400 years ago when Dutch traders on route to the Dutch East Indies (now Indonesia) at times literately collided with the State's rugged coastline, with many of their number becoming shipwrecked on what was for them a hostile and unforgiving shore. In 1829 the British proclaimed a free settlers colony on the banks of the Swan River. Today, Western Australia's outlook is very bright indeed, being a modern and vibrant State young at spirit and enthusiastic in its approach to the future.

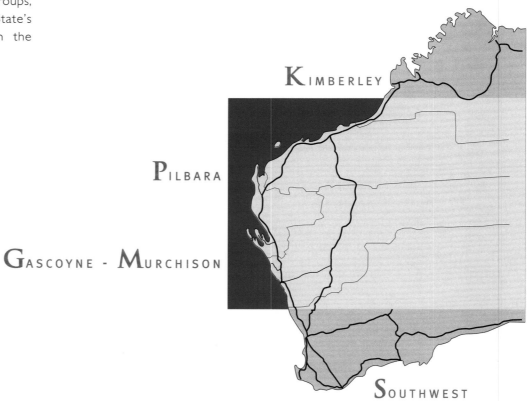

KIMBERLEY

PILBARA

GASCOYNE - MURCHISON

SOUTHWEST

CONTENTS

FOREWORD   VIII

KIMBERLEY   1

PILBARA   22

GASCOYNE - **M**URCHISON   42

SOUTHWEST   56

FOREWORD

I feel very honoured to write the foreword to this exciting collection of photographs. Having had the privilege of sharing with Greg the initial concept for this book and to now see the realisation of his vision and hard work gives me great delight.

As the pages turn we are taken through a photographic journey of Australia's biggest State, Western Australia. Greg's passion, sensitivity and sharp eye for design and colour makes this journey through the vast red and isolated North West to the beautiful but rugged southern coastline, a captivating experience.

Nature's architecture and sculpture as well as that of man have been captured with the colours of the painter's palette. Through this book, Greg has brought the panorama of Western Australia as close as our coffee table to now share with friends near or far.

Enjoy the journey of "Australia's Biggest"!

Lyn Whitfield-King M. Photog.
Australian Institute of Professional Photography

KIMBERLEY

CABLE BEACH, BROOME.

Dusk in the North West never disappoints.

A relic of the past emerges from a metallic shimmer.

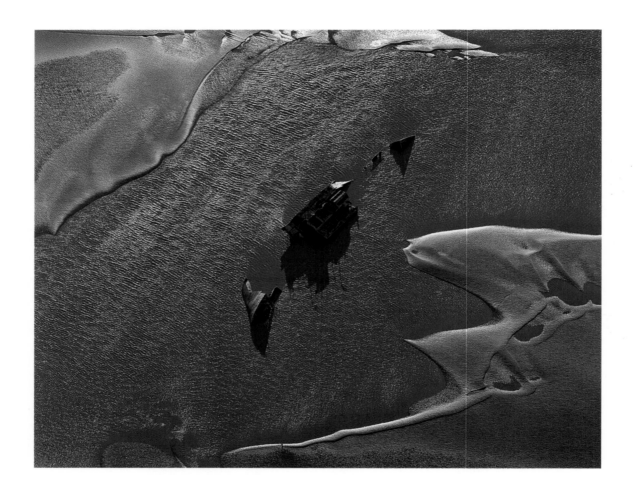

A rough corrugated exterior obscures an exciting haven for escape and enjoyment.

This laminated peninsula depicts a rugged but fragile coastline.

*Cracks and crevices characterise the identity of
this formation.*

A gigantic bolder interrupts this riverbed canyon.

Tiny tributaries penetrate sandy flats.

LAKE ARGYLE.

This man made lake holds nine times the water capacity of Sydney Harbour.

A solitary Boab acts like a guide to a rocky plateau.

P ILBARA

Carolina Creek and Pyramid Hill

Indigenous markings reveal a special past.

Clumps of spinifex emerge from a brilliant coloured bed.

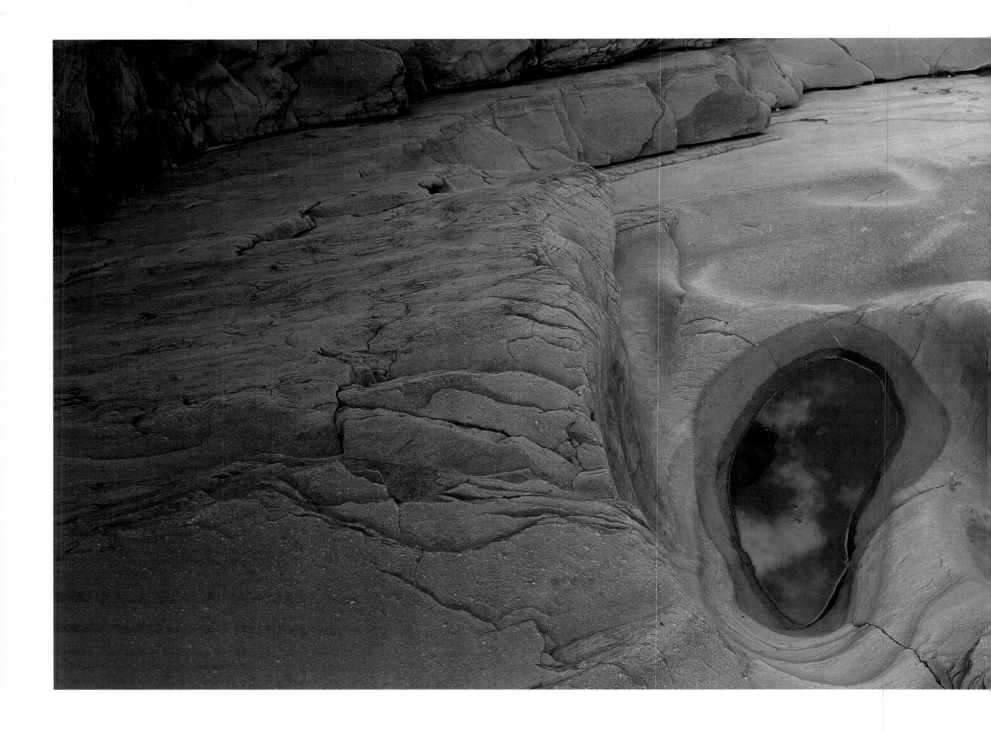

Harshness and beauty enshrine secrets of the past.

A barren valley separates spectacular ranges.

GASCOYNE—MURCHISON

BIG LAGOON, SHARK BAY.

Ocean Blues overwhelm a barren landscape.

A dusty dirt road separates special saline paddocks.

Carpets of everlastings are bathed in the last rays of the day.

THE MURCHISON RIVER, KALBARRI.

When the river flows the landscape is filled with green.

THE WORLDS BIGGEST ROCK, Mt AUGUSTUS.

*A patchwork of greens and browns gently
encompasses this majestic landform.*

These living rock like structures rest beside a tranquil shore.

Southwest

The products of thousands of tiny seeds join together
into a burst of brilliant colour.

PICTURESQUE NEW NORCIA.

Capturing a piece of Catholicism on canvas.

The illuminated metropolis stands defiant to its casual observer.

A tower of testament to lives lost and saved.

THOMSON BAY SETTLEMENT, ROTTNEST ISLAND.

Terracotta surrounds create a Mediterranean ambience.

Limestone outcrops protect sanctuary bays.

Conquering the channel — two competitors accomplish their goal.

Wind, water and waves challenge man and craft.

A spectacular Sunset filled with molten gold.

Towering defiantly as a snow capped peak.

Steel ladder to the sky.

Ornate turrets add to this unique architecture.

LAKE LEFROY, KAMBALDA.

A sliver of red earth delineates the divide between air and water.

The promise of a bright new day.

Soft glows help to mask this treacherous coastline.

LUCKY BAY, CAPE LA GRAND N.P.

Opposing granite outcrops provide an awesome entrance to this isolated bay.

A bird's eye view.

HELLFIRE BAY, CAPE LA GRAND NP.

Glistening clear blue water flanks a collection of boulders.

STIRLING RANGES.

A diverse but isolated alpine world.

A spectacle is formed at the junction of land and sea.

Energetic winds create spectacular sandscapes.

An Emu interrupts the sands of time.

COALMINE BEACH, WALPOLE.
Aqueous contours evoke a sense of peace and tranquility.

CANAL ROCKS, YELLINGUP.

Foam and spray lay undercover of a threatening sky.

SUGARLOAF ROCK, CAPE NATURALISTE.

As a blanket of darkness descends, the horizon beholds new hope.

Wind tracks provide a unique surround for this petrified sculpture.

This rocky contour creates a brilliant contrast.

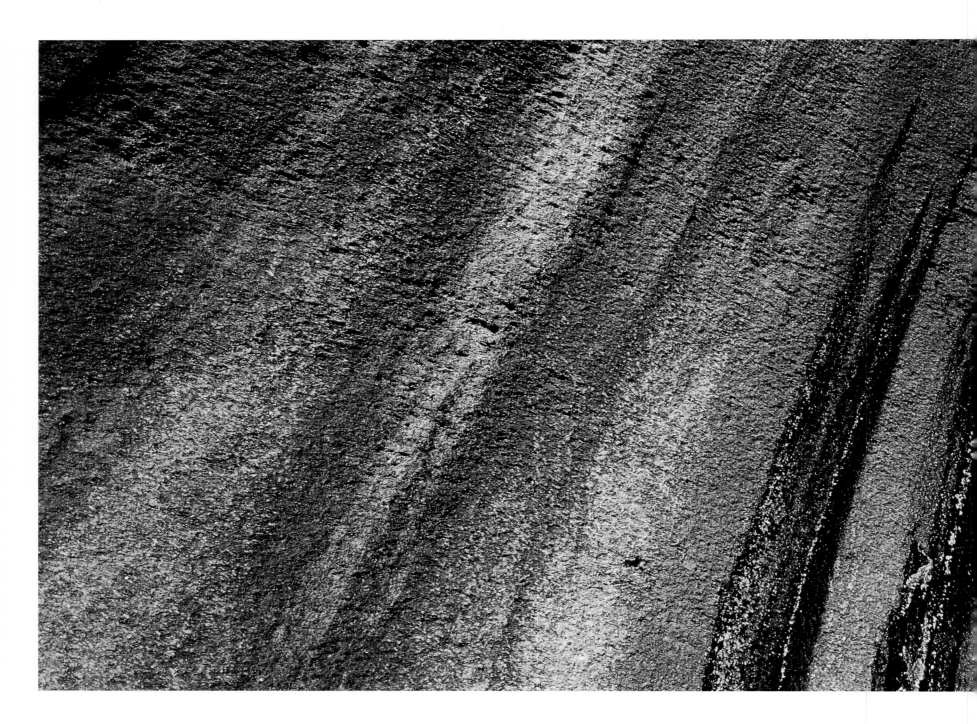

Harvested wheat forms a pinnacled landscape.

HAYSTACKS, AVON VALLEY.

Giant bales lean precariously as they defy gravity.

PHOTOGRAPHER'S NOTES

As a photographer, the ability to see the potential for a photograph in a scene and then to visualize the end picture is the true art of photography. In addition to subject matter and composition many people are interested in the technical and equipment aspects of my photography. The following is a synopsis of the film and cameras used in the production of this book.

CAMERAS

The photographs in this book have been captured on a range of different camera types. For panoramas I have used Linhof 6x17, Fuji GX 6x17, Horseman 6x12, Hasselblad Xpan and Noblex 135U cameras. When photographing from the air, I use Pentax 67, Mamiya 645 Super, Fuji GX 6x17 and Hasselblad Xpan cameras.

FILM

There are many very good film emulsions available in the market. To say that there is no one-film type right for all occasions would also be an understatement. For this book I employed the following film types: Fujichrome Velvia for the beautiful way it renders the colours of the Australian Landscape. Kodak E100VS, this film has a palette that works well for scenic photography and has the added advantage of an extra stop in speed, including very useful reciprocity characteristics for low light photography.

LIMITED EDITION PRINTS

The photographs in this book are available as limited edition décor prints. For further information please contact Greg Hocking on 08 9457 0342 or Email:altitude@ozemail.com.au

STOCK PHOTOGRAPHY

Greg Hocking is represented by Photo Index 104 Cambridge Street Leederville WA 6007 Telephone 08 9381 3466 Email:info@photoindex.com.au